strategies

FOR SUCCESS IN LAW SCHOOL AND BEYOND

The 2nd Ed. will be updated with some new narrative and new stats re law schools, etc. —

Best, Bo

strategies

FOR SUCCESS IN LAW SCHOOL AND BEYOND

CHARLES D. COLE
FRANK TOM READ
W. SCOTT SIMPSON

TATE PUBLISHING & *Enterprises*

Strategies for Success In Law School and Beyond

Published by Tate Publishing & Enterprises, LLC
127 E. Trade Center Terrace | Mustang, Oklahoma 73064 USA
1.888.361.9473 | www.tatepublishing.com

Tate Publishing is committed to excellence in the publishing industry. The company reflects the philosophy established by the founders, based on Psalm 68:11,
"The Lord gave the word and great was the company of those who published it."

Cover design by Rebekah Garibay
Interior design by Nathan Harmony

Published in the United States of America

ISBN: 978-1-61663-990-7
1. Law: General
2. Education: Professional Development
10.10.14

Acknowledgments

This book is the collaborative effort of the three authors who will be introduced to the reader in the preface that follows. All of the authors would like to acknowledge the influence that both legal education and the practical application of such has had on their lives. The system of legal education in the United States of America offered the authors the opportunity to contribute to their families and the American culture in a manner that would not have otherwise been available. Thus, the authors gratefully acknowledge the benefits they have received from the opportunity to become lawyers in America and hope that future students of the law will achieve the same personal and professional fulfillment.

Table of Contents

Foreword

This foreword provides a forum for the authors to introduce their primary contributions to the book and advise the reader of what can be expected from the material.

The authors have different perspectives about many of the issues relating to legal education in the United States. One aspect of the collective effort exhibited by the book should be recognized as supported completely by all the authors. There is a need for this book to offer information to one interested in pursuing a legal education and ultimately use such in our contemporary world. The materials are organized with four general themes. First, the reader will be given practical information throughout the book that will inform concerning both the nature of legal education and the difficulty one can experience in pursuing such. Second, advice will be offered concerning negotiating undergraduate school, which can be very helpful to one seeking admission to law school. Third, the reader will receive advice based upon the actual experience of those who have been very successful in law school concerning study methods, strategies for success in learning and sample law school exams. Fourth, and obviously important to the ultimate success of the law student who becomes a law graduate, facts concerning success in taking the bar exam and establishing a basis for participating in the legal profession will be enumerated.

Cole's primary interest is to first stress the need for the undergraduate seeking to become a lawyer to be a serious student and complete the suggested courses described in preparation for law school. Subsequent to the admonition concerning seriousness of purpose, Cole's emphasis treats how one should prepare for law classes, including offering suggestions for case briefing and preparation for law examinations. While these areas of emphasis obviously affect different times in the seven years of undergraduate and graduate matriculation, consideration of either area more than justifies the prospective lawyer's serious consideration. Cole also joins his co-authors in recognizing the grand opportunity that legal education offers to capable and interested students in the United States and recognizes that success in the legal profession is attainable if one is both capable and dedicated.

Read's primary interest, as a law school dean for twenty-nine years at five different law schools, is aiding prospective law students in selecting a law school that best fits their personal needs and career aspirations. He specifically cautions applicants to be wary of law school "rankings." Read is also concerned that the applicant, regardless of undergraduate major, takes challenging courses, particularly those that emphasize reading, writing, and speaking skills, as well as mastering courses covering difficult substantive subject matter. The better the skills set acquired in undergraduate school, the greater the chance for success in law school. Read carries this advice into law school after enrollment, urging law students to prepare for the bar examination and ultimate practice by taking difficult, basic law courses as well as courses in areas in which they think they want to practice. A broad background in all basic areas of law is helpful because law graduates frequently practice in areas that they did not anticipate when they were in law school. Read informs applicants to law school, and those applying for bar admission, of the absolute necessity of full candor on both law school and bar admission applications. Negative events in the applicant's background must be fully disclosed. Read joins his two co-authors in asserting that the study of law is fascinating—it is also hard work that requires dedication and perseverance.

Simpson's primary interest in offering the material is to emphasize the practical connection between law school studies and success in practicing law. Law is a business. The successful young lawyer needs to understand the importance of the skills learned in law school and how to advance those skills to the next level in practice life. Because the practice requires a bar license first and foremost, emphasis is placed upon bar exam preparation and the class schedule most likely to aid the prospective young lawyer in acquiring the knowledge base to prepare for the bar. Transitioning from student to practitioner is then discussed, and advice is offered on the real-world skills needed to obtain, serve, and profit from the effective representation of clients. Special emphasis is given to the successful navigation of practice life in a firm.

The reader will become aware that this material has not been written to convince one to pursue a legal education. The material seeks to advise those who desire to become lawyers of the serious dedication required of the law student to excel in both the academic and practice aspects of the profession. The legal culture of the United States demands dedication and competence from those in the profession. The serious student matriculating in law school will gain the competence and attitude to continue to learn each day in both law school and beyond. The totality of the experience will qualify the successful law student to represent others in need of legal representation and maintain the rule of law.

Preface

None of your three writers had the opportunity to read an appropriate book or talk with an experienced legal educator before attending law school. We would have benefitted if such an experience had been available. The book begins where we wish we had begun: the pre-law undergraduate experience, and then proceeds through law school, suggesting tips that will aid the reader in succeeding in that competitive academic environment. It ends with advice about achieving success on entering the practice of law. The organization of the material is intended to be relevant to each stage of the process in becoming a lawyer, and entering the profession, with advice from those who have completed the process.

A Word or Two about Your Writers

Charles D. (Bo) Cole, B.S. 1960, Auburn University; JD, cum laude, 1966, Cumberland School of Law, Samford University; LL.M. 1971, New York University; Beeson Professor of Law, Cumberland School of Law, Director, Cumberland School of Law Study-Abroad Programs and the Master of Comparative Law Program until retirement January 1, 2009. He served on the Cumberland law faculty for thirty-seven years and, during teaching sabbaticals, has practiced and worked in constitutional reform efforts, both domestically and internationally.

Frank T. (Tom) Read, universally known as Tom Read, graduated from Duke Law School in 1963. He practiced five years before returning to Duke Law School to join the faculty as Associate Dean and Professor of Law. He then went on to serve twenty-nine years as a law school dean, becoming the only person to ever serve as dean at five different ABA accredited law schools, i.e. the University of Tulsa College of Law, Indiana-Indianapolis School of Law, the University of Florida College of Law, the University of California—Hastings College of Law, and South Texas College of Law. Over the course of his twenty-nine years as a dean, Tom Read served as President of the Law School Admissions Council, Chair of the Board of Law Access, Deputy Consultant on Legal Education to the American Bar Association, and chaired or served on over fifty ABA accreditation inspections. He is currently President and Dean Emeritus at South Texas College of Law.

W. Scott Simpson, B.A. with honors, 1989, University of Florida; JD, magna cum laude, 1993, Cumberland School of Law, Samford University. Post Graduate work at the University of Alabama, Birmingham Graduate School of Business; Managing Partner of Ritchey, Simpson, Glick & Burford, PLLC. He teaches Alternative Dispute Resolution and Arbitration Law as an adjunct professor at the Cumberland School of Law. He regularly serves as an arbitrator. As an advocate, he handles arbitration cases in state and federal court throughout the United States.

The authors would like to thank Ms. Meg Flowers and Ms. Caroline Amaral for their very competent administrative aid generally and specifically in preparation of this book for publication.

Introduction

Law school is difficult, expensive and stressful! It is also one of the most exciting and challenging periods of your life. Notwithstanding those truths, a legal education continues to be both popular and highly competitive. Those with an interest in serving our culture and participating in a learned profession such as law need advice in preparing for law school and beyond. How does one prepare for law school as an undergraduate? How does one excel in law school? How do accomplished law students become successful lawyers? The purpose of this book is to offer common sense answers to those three questions.

There are many willing to offer advice concerning education generally and, specifically, pursuing a legal education and successfully practicing law. As with advice generally, one should consider the source and the experience that is the basis for the suggestions offered.

The advice that follows is from persons who have had the opportunity to observe the progress of law students, and lack of same, in law school classes during teaching adventures in excess of three decades for two of us and the continuing practice of law, as well as very successful law teaching, for one of us. Our observations and remarks are based on our personal journeys in law and our stewardship of other students and young lawyers. The suggestions that follow begin with advice for activities and planning that should occur in the potential lawyer's undergraduate efforts and selection of an appropriate law school. Specific suggestions for achieving success in law school include emphasis on study habits, class selection and preparation, student activities, work outside the law school, exam preparation, exam taking, post-exam review, and the strategy appropriate for achieving long-term educational goals. Following the emphasis on negotiating the law school experience, we will treat success in both taking the bar exam and transition from the study of law to the successful practice of law.

Our advice is based upon the writers' experiences, enhanced by currently available information. The reader should recognize, however, that the writers are not asserting that they carefully and methodically followed the advice which will be offered. In essence, this material is based upon both activities in which the writers have been involved and those that, in retrospect, they recognize would have been highly desirable. Thus, this material is offered to give the potential lawyer an opportunity to take advantage of the experiences, good and bad, of those who have already negotiated their own professional trials. The writers offer the following suggestions with the hope that they will be helpful to those considering the life-defining decision to seek a legal education and to ultimately utilize that education to serve family, legal culture, and country as a competent lawyer. There is no profession or calling that offers capable and dedicated persons an opportunity to contribute more significantly and constructively to our society than the legal profession. A well-informed approach to both planning for law school and successfully completing the law school curriculum will add to both the satisfaction obtained by the experience and the level of success achieved. The advice and suggestions herein are not intended to either persuade or dissuade the student from pursuing his or her dream. Rather, this material is offered to provide information that will be helpful in achieving one's dream.

The prospective lawyer should recognize that the decision to attend law school is one of the most consequential decisions in life. Those who undertake law school because their parents or significant others pressure them to do so, or merely to have professional standing without a serious commitment, should reconsider their long-term career interests before pursuing a legal education. A career in the legal profession can be pleasant and profitable for those who are willing to dedicate the time and effort required. A lack of dedication is fatal.

Success and satisfaction can be obtained by the law-trained individual in many constructive endeavors, not merely the traditional practice of law. Following the post-law school careers of graduates reveals that many excellent law students ultimately use their legal education in pursuits other than law practice. A legal education prepares one for careers ranging from the foreign service of the United States to real estate sales and development. Even though this material assumes most law trained persons at some point during their career will practice law, the suggestions offered are intended for application to all who aspire to be successful in law school regardless of the ultimate use of their legal education.

The decision of how to apply a legal education usually will occur after successfully completing law school and passing the bar exam. This material is designed to aid the aspiring lawyer make the best choice possible in selecting a law school, to offer reasonable suggestions for success in law school, and to offer strategies for post-law school success.

Our subject matter herein is organized in three distinct parts. First, we offer suggestions for planning undergraduate efforts aimed at admission to law school. Second, we provide advice on selecting a law school that will be best for the applicant's long-term goals. We also provide recommendations on navigating the academic requirements of the law school experience and successfully passing the bar exam. Third, we provide guidance on the critical transition from student to lawyer.

Preparation for Law School During the Undergraduate Experience

There is little doubt that the preparation for law school should commence much earlier than one's undergraduate effort. However, the reality of one's progress through life requires recognition that most of us were involved with many different types of activities in high school. Only the most unique high school student plans a professional career at that time. All life experiences influence the manner in which one makes the decision to seek a legal education. Consistent with the manner in which many students make the decision to become lawyers, we begin our advice with the undergraduate adventure.

The Road Ahead

The first degree offered by essentially all American Bar Association ("ABA") accredited law schools is that of Juris Doctor("JD"), a professional doctorate analogous to the degree obtained by medical doctors. The writers have had an opportunity during their experiences teaching law to have students in the JD programs from the US and a host of other countries. Only in the US and Canada is an undergraduate degree required prior to admission to law school. In short, an American student must complete a minimum seven years of formal education to become a lawyer—a four-year undergraduate degree and three years of law school. Elsewhere in the world, law is an undergraduate discipline that normally takes four to five years to complete. We believe the American model is superior, because law is a graduate discipline, requiring maturity and academic breadth.

There is another major difference between the civil law legal educational program and that which is offered in the US, which should be recognized. Civil law countries[1] tend to offer a more classical approach to philosophical judicial concepts than one finds in the US, where a significant emphasis is given to contemporary legal process and the practical reality of the legal profession. Further, much of civil law legal education is offered to the student on a lecture basis, while the American Bar Association accredited law schools in the US use teaching methodology which requires law student classroom participation.

Maturity and Redemption

A high level of student maturity is necessary to gain the full benefits available from the undergraduate experience. Too much partying and not enough rigorous study can (and should) preclude admission to law school. Some very intelligent students can compensate for not taking full advantage of the undergraduate academic opportunity by working extremely hard once in law school. But there is the rub: the opportunity to redeem oneself academically in law school requires that one first gain admission to law school. Thus, the first of the many suggestions for undergraduate activities for the prospective law student is simply that the student take advantage of every class in undergraduate school, master the material, and excel, building the necessary transcript for law school admission. Mark Twain allegedly stated that, "One does not get a second chance to make a first impression." Unfortunately, one does not get a second chance to master the subject matter of an undergraduate class unless one fails and re-enrolls—not a desirable alternative. Further, much more than merely passing grades are necessary for admission to a desirable law school.

Preparing for Law School Expense

One of the primary things that the prospective law student must consider during the undergraduate experience is the expense of a quality legal education. One fortunate enough to obtain a full tuition scholarship for legal education will greatly diminish the cost of the degree. Unfortunately, demand for tuition scholarships greatly exceeds the supply. Numerous qualified candidates for law school have rendered tuition scholarships much more difficult to obtain than has been the case in the past. Prospective students should commence their plans for ultimately going from undergraduate school to law school with a seriousness of purpose that is justified—not only because of the demanding nature of the law school curriculum—but, as well, the cost of matriculating in law school also must be considered.[2]

A later section of this book, treating suggestions for the selection of a law school, will offer specifics concerning the cost of law education. Undergraduate students should consider very carefully whether they wish to dedicate the extensive time and expense required for a legal education very early in their undergraduate effort. Students unwilling to dedicate themselves to the necessary time, effort, and expense should select a less-demanding profession.

A student's potential for success is increased by planning for law school early. An early commitment to become a lawyer today allows the student to select undergraduate courses that will be helpful in obtaining a quality legal education. The early commitment also will serve to motivate the student to dedicate the effort necessary to perform in an excellent manner. Admission to law school becomes more competitive every year. A mediocre academic record is insufficient to gain admission to a desirable law school.

Academic Performance in Law School

Law students today must exhibit their academic abilities from the beginning of their law school endeavors. Prospective law students must recognize that their first year grades in law school will be the prime indicator for prospective employers assessing a student's future legal performance. Bright law students who did not take undergraduate school seriously will find themselves at a disadvantage.

Law students who finish within the top 10 percent of their graduating class in ABA accredited law schools generally obtain the type of employment that they seek. Those students who do not finish within a respectable class ranking in their graduating class will find that their job opportunities are much diminished. The importance of exhibiting ones academic ability throughout his or her undergraduate career cannot be overemphasized. Demand for law graduates may suffer, like many aspects of the economy, and academic credibility is the essential ingredient for obtaining the all-important first job.

The foregoing is not to say that all students who are not sufficiently challenged in undergraduate school will not do well in law school. Few law professors, law students, or lawyers would disagree, however, that one should utilize the undergraduate experience to the maximum extent possible to develop appropriate study habits. Developing acceptable study habits and achieving general academic success in the undergraduate experience will enhance the law student's first year grades.

Desirable Undergraduate Courses

There is no "best" undergraduate major for law school. Some of the best law students we have seen are former medical doctors and professional engineers who decided to change careers. Ironically, some of the students who have had the most difficulty with law school are students who have majored in prelaw in undergraduate school. The ability and discipline of the law student seems to be the most important consideration. Even so, there are some courses which the experience of both law professors and students indicate are very helpful and should be included in the undergraduate curriculum. We offer the following suggestions for undergraduate course selection.

Analysis and Written Communication

There is little doubt that one of the primary problems that students experience in transitioning from the undergraduate school level to law school is developing both writing and analytical skills. Lawyers are problem solvers. Thus, the first year law school curriculum is dedicated to learning the language of the law and providing students with an opportunity to learn how to analyze court decisions. Students discuss and recite those cases in class. They memorialize that analysis with the written word. Hence, courses in undergraduate school that can aid the student in developing the capacity to comprehend and analyze written materials are very helpful. Any undergraduate courses offering the opportunity for students to develop the capacity to communicate in written form and engage in critical analysis are highly recommended.

Oral Communication

Courses treating voice and diction, as well as public speaking, should be completed during undergraduate school. Much law practice does not require the lawyer to speak with eloquence, contrary to the media's depiction of the profession. Lawyers, however, are expected to be in a position to express their opinion, and all law students should develop the ability to do so. More to the point, undergraduate school is a grand time to develop skills that make one's law school experience more pleasant. Many, if not most, first year law courses require the student to stand and recite assigned case material, as well as respond to the professor's questions while standing. Acceptable competence, and thus confidence, in oral communication, gained by law students during their undergraduate years, will make law school and law practice more pleasant. Lawyers who specialize in litigation must have the necessary speaking skills for a successful practice, and the same also is true of business and political leaders.

Prospective law students who enjoy the foresight to know what type of legal practice in which they will ultimately indulge can decide during undergraduate school what types of elective courses they should complete. As an example, one who aspires to practice patent law should complete the necessary engineering courses in undergraduate school to provide the technical background to make patent law practice a reality. The immediately foregoing suggestion is offered, however, with the recognition that few, very few, first year law students have specific plans to practice in a particular field of law.

American Government

Courses that relate to both the history of the American culture and governmental experience are extremely important. As our nation evolves, law students and lawyers who have an understanding of the bases for our governmental culture more readily grasp that which is and should be. Constitutional law is generally a required course in the law school curriculum and helpful to the practicing lawyer as well as the law graduate who elects to use their education in either a practice or non-practice manner. Lawyers are expected to know how to represent real people in controversies with the government and to understand government generally. An awareness of constitutional concepts limiting and granting government powers, as well as creating individual rights, is a must. Undergraduate courses treating constitutional history and general constitutional concepts should be a priority. The student should not fail, however, to revisit those concepts—in more depth—during their law school career.

Business Administration

Business courses also are important to establish an adequate foundation for law school. Prospective law students should understand basic business concepts for tax and corporate law related courses in the law school curriculum. They are then in a position to place those courses and subject matter in the proper perspective to understand a potential client's problems and help fashion appropriate solutions. Legal education, as mentioned previously, prepares one to do many things, not merely the practice of law. Most of the many potential applications of one's legal education will benefit from an understanding of business concepts, both domestically and internationally. Also, a firm understanding of financial accounting is useful in law firm management. The undergraduate experience is an excellent opportunity to begin gaining the necessary business-related background.

Language Proficiency

The use of Latin in the practice of law has been greatly diminished in contemporary America; however, a course in Latin can be very helpful to the serious law student. Current reality concerning the need for a second, and perhaps, a third language capability also should be recognized. Our country is large and grand. The wonderful characteristics of the US, with the opportunities which are present for lawyers here at home, have not created an incentive for many of us to become proficient in languages other than English. Times, however, are changing. The global economy requires that we prepare ourselves appropriately to participate in the contemporary world with proficiency in more than our native English. The prospective lawyer should take advantage of the undergraduate experience to become proficient in as many languages as time and ability allow.

■ ■ ■ ■ ■

The foregoing is not offered to indicate there is an exclusive prescriptive package of courses and undergraduate degrees which are to be preferred as a basis for those seeking to become lawyers. The above areas of emphasis, however, are considered to be very important. In all events the ability to convey one's thoughts with the written word is the most important. In selecting areas of emphasis for the undergraduate activity of students seeking to become lawyers, the following "game plan" is offered.

A "Vertical" and "Horizontal" Game Plan for Undergraduate Study

Selecting both an undergraduate major and elective courses to properly prepare you for law school requires a well thought-out game plan. One needs both vertical and horizontal planning. Here are the concepts:

Vertical Planning: Law cuts across all other occupations and disciplines. Whatever your occupation or calling, it is defined by the rules and regulations that govern it. So, the amazing truth is that no one undergraduate major is necessarily better than any other for the student to select in preparation for law school.

Examples:

- If you major in math, engineering, or one of the science disciplines, you might use that background to become a patent, trademark, or copyright attorney.
- If you major in psychology, criminal justice, or sociology, that background can aide you to become a prosecutor or criminal defense attorney.
- If you major in political science, or American history, such a major is a good background for key legal positions in governmental agencies or service at all levels of government, local, state or federal.
- If you major in economics, business, or accounting, there are a wealth of legal positions that deal with business issues, both in private and corporate practice.

And so the list goes. The Question: What should the prelaw student do? The Answer: Pick an undergraduate major in which you are truly interested and study it in depth; that is vertical study. Master your major field at a sophisticated level. Take the most challenging courses in your chosen major field and excel in them. Choose the courses that require study of difficult material and engage in complex writing projects. In short, study the field in depth; that is vertical study. By challenging yourself and your writing ability you are preparing for the rigor of law school and developing contacts with key professors that know your work and can recommend you to the law school of your choice.

Horizontal Planning: Because law cuts across all disciplines no one is ever fully prepared for the variety of legal subjects faced in a law school curriculum. As well as vertical planning (in-depth study in one challenging major as described above), you also need significant exposure to a variety of different undergraduate areas. Get a broad, general exposure to key undergraduate courses that give you critical background that can anchor you as you face the many difficult and different law courses in the first and second years of the law school curriculum.

Examples:

- Every prospective law student should have at least one course in accounting and one in basic economics because of the many areas of law practice that require a fundamental familiarity with those fields.
- A rigorous English composition course, where the papers you write are vigorously criticized, will be invaluable in all legal areas. Lawyers must be able to communicate effectively in writing.
- A good course in American government and another in American history will be helpful in many legal areas. There is an old legal adage that "an ounce of history is worth a pound of logic." In what historical and cultural climate did a particular legal rule develop? Knowing that history and the then prevailing culture can help you understand the needs the rule was created to meet.
- Lawyers also communicate in verbal forms. They negotiate, mediate, arbitrate, advise, counsel, advocate, and defend using verbal communication. Therefore a strong basic public speaking course, where you must stand on your feet and communicate, and where you will be critiqued, can be invaluable.
- The world is getting smaller, trade is becoming increasingly important, and lawyers are more and more frequently required to interact with people from other countries and cultures. Competency in another language can truly be useful in a variety of legal positions, as well as opening up legal opportunities where bilingual skills may be a prerequisite.

So . . . here are the two keys:

1. Study Vertically. Select a challenging major and then choose demanding courses within that difficult major.
2. Study Horizontally. You need a fundamental understanding of a broad variety of basic courses in a wide array of disciplines, because the range of law courses you will face requires a basic background in a multiplicity of different areas.

Prelaw Advisors

Most, if not all, undergraduate programs have prelaw advisors. The manner in which the advisor offers advice to the undergraduate student varies in undergraduate programs from merely advising those students designated as participating in a formalized prelaw program, to offering courses and scheduling advice to all undergraduate students across the curriculum, notwithstanding their major.

This latter described type of prelaw program, the advising-across-the-curriculum method, making prelaw advice available to all undergraduate students who have an interest in seeking a legal education, appears to be the current trend. The prelaw advising-across-the-curriculum seems to be imminently practical due to the fact that some aspects of the law, such as patent law, as previously mentioned, appropriately recognizes the necessity for a technical background such as engineering or chemistry, depending upon the area of patent specialty selected. Further, and perhaps more practically, one should recognize that there is a possibility that the aspiring law student will not gain admission to a law school considered to be acceptable or that the student decides, for whatever reason, that law school and legal practice is not that to which he or she would like to dedicate their lives. An undergraduate degree in business or another discipline, other than prelaw, may provide more employment opportunities and offer an understanding of numerous disciplines that will be helpful to the practicing lawyer.

The prelaw advisor can be of great aid to the undergraduate student in determining what courses to take and when to take such during the undergraduate experience. The student should seize the opportunity, as early as the undergraduate school in which one is matriculating allows, to benefit from advice to be obtained from the prelaw advisor. Many prelaw programs offer on-campus speakers and other informative programs during the undergraduate experience. The prospective law student should take advantage of all such programs that his or her academic schedule allows. Notwithstanding the benefits one can obtain from following the advice offered concerning course selection in undergraduate school and the suggested use of the prelaw advisor, all students aspiring to become lawyers in undergraduate school should continue to recognize they must excel in all courses selected in order to maximize their opportunity to be admitted to a desirable law school. Thus, selecting a major in which the aspiring law student can excel is, in many cases, the most important consideration. Grades matter! And, cultivating a superior undergraduate school grade point average ("UGPA") school is a key component to law school acceptance at a desirable school.

Employment During the Undergraduate Experience

Some law students and lawyers, both experienced and those beginning law practice, indicate that it was helpful for them to work in law offices or legally related businesses during either their college careers or following such prior to becoming a law student. Summer work for a law firm or related employment can provide a law student an opportunity to understand how demanding the legal profession can be. The practical work experience can, therefore, aid prospective law students in determining whether they are sufficiently interested in obtaining a legal education to dedicate the required large portion of their life to successfully completing law school. The writers of this material have observed that many of the more mature law students that have participated in their classes, with experience in the work-a-day world prior to entering law school, comprehend the subject-matter offered more readily than less mature students. The more mature law students also are generally sufficiently dedicated to their legal studies to excel in law school. Law study, as well as law practice, is enhanced by all of one's life experiences. Thus, work experience, to the extent such does not detract from time necessary to excel in the necessary academic work, can be very helpful before, during, and after the college years in preparing for a legal education.

Preparing for Law School Admission

The Law School Admission Test ("LSAT") is a required part of the law school admission process. The weight given the LSAT score by law school admission committees is frequently criticized by law students and some law faculty members. Nevertheless, validity studies conducted over an extended period indicate that for most law schools the LSAT is slightly more predictive of success than even the UGPA. Therefore, the prospective law student must recognize that accredited law schools give substantial weight to the LSAT scores achieved by applicants for law school.

Adequate preparation for the LSAT exam clearly relates to the manner in which the law school applicant has been dedicated to academic excellence in undergraduate school. Additionally, however, students must be aware that courses and materials are available that are designed to prepare the law school applicant for the examination. The writers of these materials have no financial interest in LSAT preparation courses or materials and lament the fact that the best formal preparation courses are expensive. Unfortunately, however, admission to ABA accredited law schools has become so competitive that the prospective law student should take a substantive

LSAT preparatory course and treat the same very seriously. A less than excellent LSAT score may be offset somewhat in the admission process by an excellent undergraduate transcript; however, the law school applicant should avoid relying upon that strategy if at all possible. This material will offer additional, more specific, information concerning the LSAT in the portion that follows treating law school admission criteria.

An excellent score on the LSAT test is, as described above, highly desirable to make the student's application to law school viable; however, many argue the most relevant indication of sufficient intelligence and discipline to succeed in law school is the student's UGPA. The prospective law student should look upon every course in undergraduate school, with special emphasis on the writing courses, as stair-steps to the ultimate goal. The goal—admission and success in the law school of the student's choice—is attainable. Prospective law students can look about their hometowns and in state and federal governments to those persons who have successfully completed their legal educations. Those lawyers considered are generally bright and dedicated; thus, they are successful. Most prospective law students are also bright and dedicated. However, they must not fail to exhibit both their intellectual capacity and dedication to achieve the opportunity to serve our society and their families as lawyers. The undergraduate experience, when indicative of a bright and motivated student, translates into a competitive LSAT score, as well as an enviable UGPA.

Develop a Long-term Plan for Law School Success

Throughout the undergraduate experience, the prospective law student must continue to recognize the competitiveness of the law school admission process and consistently seek to achieve the highest academic results possible in all courses. Also of paramount importance, the prospective law student must develop the necessary long-term plan to achieve the goal he or she has established, including how the cost of a legal education will be covered. A law student should not undertake the rigors of a legal education without planning properly for the expense of both living appropriately during law school and covering the actual costs for tuition and books. The expense that is anticipated should include adequate housing, transportation, health insurance, and other day-to-day living expenses.

The writers of this material have observed many bright young law students over the years that have placed themselves in untenable circumstances by not identifying the necessary financial resources to cover their legal education before entering law school. Some of the students in question have given up their dream to become a lawyer completely. Others have dropped out of law school and worked to create the necessary funds and returned to law school when financial resources were available. The prospective law student should avoid this trauma by planning prior to commencing the law school experience.

The law school plan, in addition to the previous suggestions, should also consider both the geographical area in which the student would like to practice and the type practice he or she would like to pursue. Law students develop life-long friendships with their class colleagues throughout their law school tenure. The experience of most practicing lawyers indicates that practicing in the geographical area in which one attended law school can be important to the success and satisfaction enjoyed from practice. All of the enumerated concerns above, among others, are relevant to determine generally which law schools would be best for the individual student and how the student should plan law school matriculation to avoid increasing the stress that will occur due to lack of adequate funds during the legal education experience.

One additional, important factor relating to preparation of the undergraduate who aspires to become a lawyer must be recognized. Most of us, as undergraduate students, have been involved in activities that were embarrassing at the time and we later regret. A bit too much beer or a personal encounter which led to a confrontation and ultimately a misdemeanor conviction or other breach of the peace problem will be reviewed carefully by the law school admission committee and the applicable state bar association when one seeks to take the bar exam. Obviously, the best advice which can be given and acted upon would be to avoid any such activities. Further, the application for law school admission and application to sit for the bar examination both require that all infractions must be explicitly divulged. Tell the truth! Attempted deception is much worse than complete truth that, generally, is subject to satisfactory explanation. Even an unintentional lapse of memory and failure to list prior legal infractions can require the law school applicant to amend the admission application and appear before a character and fitness committee of the law school or bar association.

Selecting the Law School That Will Be Best for the Applicant's Long-term Goals

Selecting a law school for one's legal education may be determined by simply finding a law school that will accept the applicant. In all events, if at all possible, the law school selected should be an ABA accredited school and highly regarded in the geographical area most appropriate for the law student. The information which follows assumes that the prospective law student has taken advantage of the undergraduate experience and has a sufficient UGPA and LSAT score to have reasonable expectations that an appropriate law school admission is probable, if not assured.

Law School Rankings

The law school selection process discussed recognizes that different ABA approved law schools have different admission requirements. Thus, if the student has a UGPA in the B to B+ category and an LSAT score in the 155–159 range, it will be more than merely difficult for the applicant to be accepted by that which is recognized as a "top tier" nationally recognized law school. The often maligned, and perhaps over-emphasized, "US News and World Report Rankings of America's Best Graduate Schools," provides rankings and data available for the 194 ABA law schools that are accredited each year.[3]

Yale University law school, generally recognized as one of the best law schools in America, has often been ranked as the number one law school in the US.[4] The UGPA and LSAT average score for Yale's entering class, as well as the statistics for other highly ranked law schools, are reported in the previously cited US News and World Report article and are available for the interested student on an annual basis.

Baylor University School of Law, generally ranked much lower than Yale by the same methodology and types of data , had a higher bar passage rate than Yale during a recent reporting period . Baylor's UGPA and LSAT average score for the entering class in question was remarkably lower than the same statistics for Yale's entering class. Obviously one could treat national rankings as a basis for some comparison; however, when doing so it is interesting to note that Georgia State University's law school, ranked lower than either Yale or Baylor by several organizations that offer law school comparisons, on the same types of data and using the same methodology for the same time-frame, reported a bar passage rate more than competitive with Baylor. Interestingly, Georgia State University's law school reported a UGPA lower than Baylor for the entering class and a compatible LSAT average during the year in question.

One must certainly recognize that there are numerous variables in comparing data and law school quality, such as the state wherein the bar exam is administered, the policies of the bar examiners in the state, and among others, the philosophy of the bar examiners as exhibited in their tests and grading. One should further understand, however, how a casual overview of the rankings can be considered by some, including law school faculties and administrators, to be subject to being misconstrued. Prospective law students interested in reviewing law school rankings should see the most current US News and World Report article mentioned above, the report of the Internet Legal Research Group[5] and The Princeton Review.[6]

An article in the ABA Journal treating the concerns expressed by numerous law deans throughout the US is helpful in identifying some of the primary concerns with the US News and World Report rankings. The article, "The Rankings Law Deans Hate,"[7] notes that the rankings were first offered for publication in 1987 and are often attacked as based upon methodology that is "easily manipulated and too subjective to carry such inordinate weight."[8]

In response, Robert Morse, the gentleman who created and compiles the law school rankings:

> Thinks it is others [not him] who invest the rankings with greater importance than they deserve. He defends them, neither as calculus nor social science, but as an honestly derived "guide."[9]

Mr. Morse is further quoted as stating that:

> Any student or parent who uses the rankings as the No. 1 reason to go to a school, well, that's exactly the wrong way to use them. The rankings are a tool. They give deans and students useful statistics for comparisons.[10]

A detailed analysis of available law school rankings is beyond the scope of this material. One should recognize, however, that the rankings do exist and are available for prospective law students to review should they so desire. Even a casual observer will readily recognize that the more selective the law school the more difficult admission becomes. Further, very importantly, the prospective law student should recognize that qualities that make one kind of law school good for one student may not be as important to another.[11]

The average applicant[12] should not despair. Law schools are available for applicants considered to be average which offer the opportunity for an excellent legal education. One must continue to recognize, however, that the more prestigious the law school one attends the more initial opportunities which will generally be available to its graduates. Although students should seek admission to the "best" law school available, they must be realistic. Being realistic requires that one apply to several law schools if the applicant is in the "average" student range. Further, the law schools selected for applications should be within the range of the individual applicant's qualifications. The prospective law student should use available literature and information obtained on the Internet Web page of law schools in which the student has an interest to identify the law schools for application purposes.[13]

Assuming that the student is realistic and seeks to be admitted to an appropriate law school, the following subject areas, among others, must be considered. The admission criteria for law schools in which the students have an interest are obviously very important. Next, one must consider the cost for legal education at each of the schools in which there is an interest, including scholarship support available from each school and, perhaps, available convenient employment in the geographical area in which the law school is located. The emphasis of the law school should also be considered, i.e., some law schools emphasize their trial practice programs while others may emphasize, among other areas of emphasis, international or comparative law. The law student, however, should not expect to obtain a legal specialty while obtaining the first degree in law school. Academic legal specialties are available to law graduates in post-graduate programs, normally when one seeks a Master of Law ("LL.M") degree. The student can expect a greater emphasis for the subject courses available in the areas that the law school asserts as its "claim to fame" or academic emphasis. While the opportunity to progress to an LL.M at the law school where one obtains the JD degree may be important to the individual student for personal preference reasons, many legal educators assert that exposure to another ABA approved law school for graduate work can be academically rewarding.

Practical considerations such as the geographical area where one would like ultimately to practice or work in a law-related professional position is important. Graduates from law schools who enjoy an excellent reputation within the geographical area in which the law school is located tend to receive priority for hiring purposes over graduates from more distant areas or from law schools in the geographic area that does not enjoy a competitively excellent reputation. The student also may wish to undertake the serious commitment to legal education, most likely the first legal degree, within a close proximity to one's home. While young, we tend to look at the three-year law school experience as a short time. Unfortunately, the law student is generally of the age where many families have reached the point in life when physical health problems begin to occur. Over the years of law school teaching, we have heard numerous students lament that they are too far from their family to be of emotional aid to them. This potential problem also is true in reverse. The law student requires emotional support from his or her family. The recognition that an appropriate geographical location should be considered offers the additional benefit of attending law school in an area in which the student intends to practice. Such an approach also will contribute to establishing contacts during law school that can be very helpful in establishing a viable client base.

The foregoing enumerated concerns deserve individual consideration and will be discussed separately.

Admission Criteria for Law Schools

The two most important criteria for admission to any ABA accredited law school, as previously mentioned, are the LSAT and the UGPA.

The LSAT

The LSAT score is required for admission by all ABA accredited law schools in the United States and by Canadian Law Schools as well. It tests, among other skills, the twin critical abilities of reading comprehension and analytical ability. All applicants take the same test, thus law schools can compare the critical learning skills of every applicant against those of all other applicants. The LSAT has great predictive ability as to the applicant's prospective first year law school grades. As with all standardized tests, it does not measure critical human qualities such as integrity, motivation and diligence. The LSAT score has a "six-point standard error-of-measurement." In short, if an applicant receives a 155 score, the correct score is somewhere in the band between 152 to 158. So an informed admissions committee reads the correct score as being somewhere between that six-point range. As indicated, the LSAT is the single best predictor of a law student's first year academic performance and is, therefore, of great importance in the admissions process.

The UGPA

Obviously, logic indicates the best predictor of overall future academic success is past undergraduate academic success. Thus, the four-year undergraduate academic record, the UGPA, is the second critical factor in making the law school admissions decision. Nevertheless, there are two factors which affect the ability of an applicant's UGPA to truly predict the applicant's law school performance. The first issue is how long ago was the undergraduate academic record completed? The further in the past the undergraduate years are, the less predictive the applicant's UGPA will be. The second problem is the vast variety of undergraduate grading systems used in America's 2,500 undergraduate institutions. What is the system? Have grades been inflated in that system? In some undergraduate schools, a particular major—say political science—may be rigorously evaluated while in another institution, political science may be considered to be a very easy major, not evaluated with rigor at all. Comparing UGPA's for applicants from a multiplicity of different undergraduate institutions is frequently like comparing apples to oranges. It is a very idiosyncratic task. This difficulty partially explains why the LSAT, which is uniform to all applicants, is so important to law schools.

Other Criteria for Law School Admission

While impossible to quantify, like the LSAT and UGPA, other criteria can be influential with a law school's admission committee. A recommendation letter from an undergraduate professor with real insight into an applicant's abilities can be persuasive. Letters from family friends are not so helpful. Other academic work at the graduate level can enhance an application. A strong, well-written personal statement detailing life experiences and aspirations will be helpful. If the law school allows a personal, on-site interview, take advantage of the opportunity. You will learn about the school, and they will know your interest is real. In a close admissions case, these non-quantifiable portions of the application can be critical to the ultimate decisions made on a particular applicant.

Expense of Legal Education

Legal education in accredited law schools of the United States and Canada is, in the opinion of the writers of this material, the best legal education system available anywhere in our modern world. One must recognize that the expense of a quality legal educational system is a major concern. The total expense applicable to legal education must include the time spent to successfully matriculate the three year curriculum for the basic JD degree, the cost of living during the law school term including housing, medical insurance, and other general expenses, as well as tuition and books (both tuition and books become more expensive every year). Law students should be aware that university dorms are not generally available for law students. Unmarried law students should consider finding a compatible roommate, and all law students should make every effort to live reasonably but frugally during their law school tenure.[14]

As one would surmise, private law schools—those not part of a state-funded school system—offer the most expensive legal educations. The public law schools—those that are state supported—are the most economical for a resident of the state in which the state law school is located. The cost for out-of-state residents to attend a state law school corresponds somewhat to the cost of attending private law schools within the state in question.

Loans are readily available to pay tuition and living expenses. It is recommended that a student first seek federally insured loans because of longer repayment periods and lower interest rates. However, there is a rather modest limit on how much you can borrow from federally insured sources. Many students, therefore, are forced to seek additional loan funding from other sources. Such private loans have been readily available because of a record of high repayment by law students. The risk, of course, is that too high a loan balance from too many loan sources can be a great burden on a young lawyer just getting started in practice. Paying law school debts can stretch over many years and is roughly the equivalent of paying off a second mortgage. Seek sound advice before undertaking major debt obligations; every law school provides its students access to sound financial advice through a financial aid office. Prior to graduation, it is wise to obtain information on consolidating loans and extending the repayment periods. By all means, avoid high credit card debt at high interest rates; too much credit card debt can pave the road to financial disaster.

These materials previously used the law schools of Yale University, Baylor University and Georgia State University for examples of LSAT and GPA admission requirements, with reference to law school rankings and bar passage rates of the three law schools.[15] The material that follows the text of this book as Appendix A will use the same three law schools to offer tuition cost information. Appendix A also includes the state law school of the University of Alabama and a private law school within the State of Alabama, Cumberland School of Law, Samford University, for tuition comparison purposes. Additionally, the student should recognize that a total estimated annual cost must include other fees and living expenses. The Web sites for most ABA approved law schools provide additional information, which will be helpful in estimating total annual expense.

All cost comparisons, as well as other attributes of the schools selected for comparison and the remaining ABA approved law schools can be found in the ABA LSAC Official Guide to ABA-Approved Law Schools.[16] Another recognized source of obtaining excellent information concerning ABA approved law schools, The Princeton Review,[17] also should be recognized. The methodology used to obtain the information published in The Princeton Review is quoted from the Review's website as:

> [T]he Princeton Review surveyed more than 18,000 students at 170 law schools and used the information that they reported to us, along with school statistics provided by school administrators, to create 11 ranking lists. None of these lists purports to rank the schools in terms of overall quality; but by using the lists in conjunction with the Students Say profiles and the school statistics, you will be able to identify the attributes of a law school that are important to you—and ultimately, generate a list of schools that can best help you achieve your personal and professional goals. [18]

Alternatives to Full-Time On-Site Legal Education

Some states of the US offer an alternative to the law school experience. Notably, California, Maine, New York, Vermont, Virginia, Washington, and Wyoming allow forms of apprenticeships, generally called "reading the law."[19] There are obvious benefits and detriments to use of a legal education system that existed before radio, television, telephone, the Internet, and a myriad of other innovations in the American fabric of life. Such alternatives are rarely used and considered much inferior to the classical law school experience. This material concentrates upon the generally accepted manner of obtaining the privilege to represent others in our legal and social culture. The "generally accepted manner" to which this text refers is the three-year curriculum wherein the students participate to the best of their ability in the classroom with fellow law students.

The foregoing described approach to offer a baseline description of law schools, in which legal education is effectively offered in the US, also is not without recognition of the current availability of an "online" Internet legal education. Distance learning, as well as hands-on apprenticeships and variations of the law school curriculum as it currently exists in the ABA approved law schools, provides much food for thought; however, those considerations are beyond the scope of this material for suggested legal education in contemporary America. The previous material concerning alternatives to obtaining a legal education is mentioned merely to inform the reader of the availability of such alternatives. The experience and observations of the writers of this material favors traditional legal education as it has evolved in the majority of states of the US. The current system for legal education in the US is not perfect. Improvements can and will occur to the system in the future.[20] However, the prospective lawyer should take advantage of the excellence of the current system in an ABA approved law school that is the best "fit" for the individual law student. One should recognize that the learning process includes learning from and with class colleagues, not merely the understanding of information read or viewed. Further, one should get the benefit of establishing long-term professional and personal relationships with one's colleagues during the law school experience.

Specific Suggestions for Achieving Success in Law School

Just as there are benefits to planning one's undergraduate efforts to facilitate being admitted to law school, planning is imperative to aid the law school student to perform in an outstanding manner in law school. US law schools begin the first year experience with varying types of orientation programs. The new student has the opportunity to become acquainted with the physical plant of the law school, including classrooms, and very importantly, the library, as well as obtain information concerning class preparation and law faculty expectations. Faculty, as well as representative second- and third-year students, may make presentations to the entering first year students ("1Ls"). The information offered may seem too simple or too complex to be of any aid. Such is not the case. Entering students should attend all sessions and begin to make friends with as many of the other 1Ls as possible. The law school colleagues, fellow students, with whom the student is going to spend both class and study time over the next three years, are the first in-school support system the student must have.

Competition among students for grades and recognition will occur during the course of the law school experience. Even so, law students who develop friendships with fellow students enjoy their law school career more than "loner" students and generally continue to have close relationships with their classmates throughout their professional careers. The friendships and personal relationships that the law student experience develops—with both faculty and student colleagues—will be valuable throughout one's legal career. Therefore, one should take maximum advantage of the orientation program to obtain the most benefit possible from every aspect of the program and create constructive friendships with fellow students, administrative staff of the law school, and law faculty.

The law school classes usually will be conducted in a manner that is called a Socratic or Socratic/lecture method, described also as the dialectic or modified Socratic method. The classic Socratic method would have the professor answer questions with questions; however, the number of students in law classes and the amount of material necessary to be covered in law classes in our contemporary world does not generally allow such an approach. Law classes generally proceed today with a modified Socratic method. Questions are used by the professor to delve into the subject of the assignment, normally preceded with a short lecture or appropriate comment concerning the material.

Students are expected to prepare assigned material for discussion and presentation. The assigned material normally includes edited cases in casebooks treating the subject matter for each course, both required courses and electives. The student is generally called upon to recite one of the edited cases assigned, and the professor then asks questions concerning the case and offers materials to sum up the area of law treated by the case or cases discussed.

The student learns to analyze the cases assigned. This procedure offers an opportunity to become proficient in both the analysis and the method of writing the "brief"[21] of the case for class recitation. Briefing is somewhat baffling at first to many, if not most, entering law students. Thus, these materials will offer examples of edited cases and the manner in which the student should analyze, or brief, cases assigned for class purposes. The sample cases and a written brief with comments following each, with specific suggestions for class preparation, are offered infra.

Sample Constitutional Law Case

The case selected for our constitutional law sample case is Skinner v. Oklahoma.[22] The edited version set forth below was prepared by one of the authors for a comparative constitutional law course.[23] The student will note that the case name is followed by the page number in the casebook from which it is taken because the student should be in a position to access the opinion from the class materials assigned for maximum effectiveness in class notes and, ultimately, the student prepared course outline that will be highly recommended in the materials that follow concerning class and exam preparation.

Sample Brief

Skinner v. Oklahoma, Supreme Court of the US, p. 182 (1942). Mr. Justice Douglas delivered the opinion of the Court.

This case touches a sensitive and important area of human rights. Oklahoma deprives certain individuals of a right that is basic to the perpetuation of a race—the right to have offspring. Oklahoma has decreed the enforcement of its law against petitioner, overruling his claim that it violated the Fourteenth Amendment [of the US Constitution]. Because that decision raised grave and substantial constitutional questions, we granted the petition for certiorari.

The statute involved is Oklahoma's Habitual Criminal Sterilization Act. That Act defines a "habitual criminal" as a person who, having been convicted two or more times for crimes "amounting to felonies involving moral turpitude," either in an Oklahoma court or in a court of any other State, is thereafter convicted of such a felony in Oklahoma and is sentenced to a term of imprisonment in an Oklahoma penal institution. Machinery is provided for the institution by the attorney general of a proceeding against such a person in the Oklahoma courts for a judgment that such person shall be rendered sexually sterile. Notice, an opportunity to be heard, and the right to a jury trial are provided. The issues triable in such a proceeding are narrow and confined. If the court or jury finds that the defendant is a "habitual criminal" and that he "may be rendered sexually sterile without detriment to his or her general health," then the court "shall render judgment to the effect that said defendant be rendered sexually sterile" by the operation of [a] vasectomy in case of a male, and of [a] salpingectomy in case of a female. Only one other provision of the Act is material here, and that is § 195, which provides that "offenses arising out of the violation of the prohibitory laws, revenue acts, embezzlement, or political offenses, shall not come or be considered within the terms of this Act."

Petitioner was convicted in 1926 of the crime of stealing chickens and was sentenced to the Oklahoma State Reformatory. In 1929, he was convicted of the crime of robbery with firearms and was sentenced to the reformatory. In 1934, he was convicted again of robbery with firearms and was sentenced to the penitentiary. He was confined there in 1935, when the Act was passed. In 1936, the attorney general instituted proceedings against him. Petitioner in his answer challenged the Act as unconstitutional by reason of the Fourteenth Amendment. A jury trial was had. The court instructed the jury that the crimes of which petitioner had been convicted were felonies involving moral turpitude, and that the only question for the jury was whether the operation of vasectomy could be performed on petitioner without detriment to his general health. The jury found that it could be. A judgment directing that the operation of vasectomy be performed on petitioner was affirmed by the Supreme Court of Oklahoma by a five to four decision.

Several objections to the constitutionality of the Act have been pressed upon us. It is urged that the Act cannot be sustained as an exercise of the police power, in view of the state of scientific authorities respecting inheritability of criminal traits. It is argued that due process is lacking because, under this Act, unlike the Act upheld in Buck v. Bell, 274 US 200, the defendant is given no opportunity to be heard on the issue as to whether he is the probable potential parent of socially undesirable offspring. It is also suggested that the Act is penal in character and that the sterilization provided for is cruel and unusual punishment and violative of the Fourteenth Amendment. We pass those points without intimating an opinion on them, for there is a feature of the Act that clearly condemns it. That is, its failure to meet the requirements of the equal protection clause of the Fourteenth Amendment.

We do not stop to point out all of the inequalities in this Act. A few examples will suffice. In Oklahoma, grand larceny is a felony. Larceny is grand larceny when the property taken exceeds twenty dollars in value. Embezzlement is punishable "in the manner prescribed for feloniously stealing property of the value of that embezzled." Hence, he who embezzles property worth more than twenty dollars is guilty of a felony. A clerk who appropriates over twenty dollars from his employer's till and a stranger who steals the same amount are thus both guilty of felonies. If the latter repeats his act and is convicted three times, he may be sterilized. But the clerk is not subject to the pains and penalties of the Act no matter how large his embezzlements nor how frequent his convictions. A person who enters a chicken coop and steals chickens commits a felony, and he may be sterilized if he is thrice convicted. If, however, he is a bailee of the property and fraudulently appropriates it, he is an embezzler.

Hence, no matter how habitual his proclivities for embezzlement are and no matter how often his conviction, he may not be sterilized. Thus, the nature of the two crimes is intrinsically the same [but] they are [not] punishable in the same manner. Furthermore, the line between them follows close distinctions—distinctions comparable to those highly technical ones which shaped the common law as to "trespass" or "taking." There may be larceny by fraud rather than embezzlement, even where the owner of the personal property delivers it to the defendant, if the latter has at that time "a fraudulent intention to make use of the possession as a means of converting such property to his own use, and does so convert it." If the fraudulent intent occurs later and the defendant converts the property, he is guilty of embezzlement. Whether a particular act is larceny by fraud or embezzlement thus turns not on the intrinsic quality of the act but on when the felonious intent arose—a question for the jury under appropriate instructions.

It was stated in Buck v. Bell, supra, that the claim that state legislation violates the equal protection clause of the Fourteenth Amendment is "the usual last resort of constitutional arguments." Under our constitutional system the States in determining the reach and scope of particular legislation need not provide "abstract symmetry." They may mark and set apart the classes and types of problems according to the needs and as dictated or suggested by experience. It was in that connection that Mr. Justice Holmes, speaking for the Court in Bain Peanut Co. v. Pinson, 282 US 499, 501, stated, "[W]e must remember that the machinery of government would not work if it were not allowed a little play in its joints." Only recently we reaffirmed the view that the equal protection clause does not prevent the legislature from recognizing "degrees of evil" by our ruling in Tigner v. Texas, 310 US 141, 147, that "the Constitution does not require things that are different in fact or opinion to be treated in law as though they were the same." Thus, if we had here only a question as to a State's classification of crimes, such as embezzlement or larceny, no substantial federal question would be raised. For a State is not constrained in the exercise of its police power to ignore experience which marks a class of offenders or a family of offenses for special treatment. Nor is it prevented by the equal protection clause from confining "its restrictions to those classes of cases where the need is deemed to be clearest." As stated in Buck v. Bell, supra, p. 208, "... the law does all that is needed when it does all that it can, indicates a policy, applies it to all within the lines, and seeks to bring within the lines all similarly situated so far and so fast as its means allow."

But the instant legislation runs afoul of the equal protection clause, though we give Oklahoma that large deference, which the rule of the foregoing cases requires. We are dealing here with legislation that involves one of the basic civil rights of man. Marriage and procreation are fundamental to the very existence and survival of the race. The power to sterilize, if exercised, may have subtle, far-reaching, and devastating effects. In evil or reckless hands, it can cause races or types that are inimical to the dominant group to wither and disappear. There is no redemption for the individual whom the law touches. Any experiment that the State conducts is to his irreparable injury. He is forever deprived of a basic liberty. We mention these matters not to reexamine the scope of the police power of the States. We advert to them merely in emphasis of our view that strict scrutiny of the classification that a State makes in a sterilization law is essential, lest unwittingly, or otherwise, invidious discriminations are made against groups or types of individuals in violation of the constitutional guaranty of just and equal laws. The guaranty of "equal protection of the laws is a pledge of the protection of equal laws." Yick Wo v. Hopkins, 118 US 356, 369. When the law lays an unequal hand on those who have committed intrinsically the same quality of offense and sterilizes one and not the other, it has made as invidious a discrimination as if it had selected a particular race or nationality for oppressive treatment. Yick Wo v. Hopkins, supra; Gaines v. Canada, 305 US 337. Sterilization of those who have thrice committed grand larceny, with immunity for those who are embezzlers is a clear, pointed, unmistakable discrimination. Oklahoma makes no attempt to say that he who commits larceny by trespass, or trick, or fraud has biologically inheritable traits that he who commits embezzlement lacks. Oklahoma's line between larceny by fraud and embezzlement is determined, as we have noted, "with reference to the time when the fraudulent intent to convert the property to the taker's own use" arises. We have not the slightest basis for inferring that that line has any significance in eugenics, nor that the inheritability of criminal traits follows the neat legal distinctions that the law has marked between those two offenses. In terms of fines and imprisonment, the crimes of larceny and embezzlement rate the same under the Oklahoma code. Only when it comes to sterilization are the pains and penalties of the law different. The equal protection clause would indeed be a formula of empty words if such conspicuously artificial lines could be drawn. In Buck v. Bell, supra, the Virginia statute was upheld though it applied only to feeble-minded persons in institutions of the State. But it was pointed out that "so far as the operations enable those who otherwise must be kept confined to be returned to the world, and thus open the asylum to others, the equality aimed at will be more nearly reached." Here there is no such saving feature. Embezzlers are forever free. Those who steal or take in other ways are not. If such a classification were permitted, the technical common law concept of a "trespass" based on distinctions that are "very largely dependent upon history for explanation" could readily become a rule of human genetics.

It is true that the Act has a broad severability clause. But we will not endeavor to determine whether its application would solve the equal protection difficulty. The Supreme Court of Oklahoma sustained the Act without reference to the severability clause. We have therefore a situation where the Act as construed and applied to petitioner is allowed to perpetuate the discrimination that we have found to be fatal. Whether the severability clause would be so applied as to remove this particular constitutional objection is a question that may be more appropriately left for adjudication by the Oklahoma court. That is reemphasized here by our uncertainty as to what excision, if any, would be made as a matter of Oklahoma law. It is by no means clear whether, if an excision were made, this particular constitutional difficulty might be solved by enlarging on the one hand or contracting on the other the class of criminals who might be sterilized.

Reversed.

Mr. Chief Justice Stone, concurring:[24]

I concur in the result, but I am not persuaded that we are aided in reaching it by recourse to the equal protection clause.

If Oklahoma may resort generally to the sterilization of criminals on the assumption that their propensities are transmissible to future generations by inheritance, I seriously doubt that the equal protection clause requires it to apply the measure to all criminals in the first instance, or to none.

Moreover, if we must presume that the legislature knows—what science has been unable to ascertain—that the criminal tendencies of any class of habitual offenders are transmissible regardless of the varying mental characteristics of its individuals, I should suppose that we must likewise presume that the legislature, in its wisdom, knows that the criminal tendencies of some classes of offenders are more likely to be transmitted than those of others. And so I think the real question we have to consider is not one of equal protection, but whether the wholesale condemnation of a class to such an invasion of personal liberty, without opportunity to any individual to show that his is not the type of case which would justify resort to it, satisfies the demands of due process.

There are limits to the extent to which the presumption of constitutionality can be pressed, especially where the liberty of the person is concerned (Carolene Products Co., 304 US 144, 152, n.4) and where the presumption is resorted to only to dispense with a procedure which the ordinary dictates of prudence would seem to demand for the protection of the individual from arbitrary action. Although petitioner here was given a hearing to ascertain whether sterilization would be detrimental to his health, he was given none to discover whether his criminal tendencies are of an inheritable type. Undoubtedly, a state may, after appropriate inquiry, constitutionally interfere with the personal liberty of the individual to prevent the transmission by inheritance of his socially injurious tendencies. Buck v. Bell, 274 US 200. But until now we have not been called upon to say that it may do so without giving him a hearing and opportunity to challenge the existence as to him of the only facts that could justify so drastic a measure.

Science has found and the law has recognized that there are certain types of mental deficiency associated with delinquency that are inheritable. But the State does not contend—nor can there be any pretense—that either common knowledge or experience, or scientific investigation, has given assurance that the criminal tendencies of any class of habitual offenders are universally or even generally inheritable. In such circumstances, inquiry whether such is the fact in the case of any particular individual cannot rightly be dispensed with. Whether the procedure by which a statute carries its mandate into execution satisfies due process is a matter of judicial cognizance. A law that condemns without hearing all the individuals of a class to so harsh a measure as the present because some, or even many, merit condemnation is lacking in the first principles of due process. And so, while the state may protect itself from the demonstrably inheritable tendencies of the individual that are injurious to society, the most elementary notions of due process would seem to require it to take appropriate steps to safeguard the liberty of the individual by affording him, before he is condemned to an irreparable injury in his person, some opportunity to show that he is without such inheritable tendencies. The state is called on to sacrifice no permissible end when it is required to reach its objective by a reasonable and just procedure adequate to safeguard rights of the individual which concededly the Constitution protects.

The concurrence of Mr. Justice Jackson is omitted.

■ ■ ■ ■ ■

The Skinner case is an interesting constitutional law case that presents an Equal Protection Clause[25] question. The reader should recognize that the substantive law of equal protection is the basis for the Court's opinion. Thus, a bit of background concerning the concepts involved to understand the opinion should be offered before a sample "brief" for law school purposes is offered.

The equal protection concept in the US Constitution requires that all persons similarly situated should be treated in a similar manner. When the governmental regulation is an infringement of a right the Court has recognized as fundamental[26] for protection purposes the Court does not defer to the law maker, it strictly reviews the governmental purpose or effect. The state, Oklahoma, authorized a sterilization of habitual criminals, those who thrice have been convicted of a felony involving moral turpitude. The state statute provided for a very narrow judicial review during the hearing to determine if sterilization should occur, the narrow question to be considered was whether the habitual criminal could be sexually sterilized without detriment to his or her general health. This narrow scope of judicial review, the basis for Chief Justice Stone's concurrence, indicates a lack of procedural due process. Procedural due process requires that one be given a fair procedure, notice and an opportunity to be heard on issues affecting one's life, liberty, or property.[27] The concurrence is interesting; however, one should recognize that the binding precedent is based upon the majority opinion of the Court. An opinion of the Court, to be binding precedent, must be based upon an opinion in which a majority of the justices (generally five of the nine) agree both to the reason the Court decides the case and the judgment rendered.

A careful reading of the edited opinion of the Skinner case will reveal that the defendant's counsel sought to have the court decide the appeal on the basis that the defendant was not given the opportunity to be heard on the issue of whether the defendant was the probable potential parent of socially undesirable offspring, a lack of procedural due process. Justice Douglas' majority opinion, however, used the Equal Protection Clause to decide the case, recognizing that the right to procreate was fundamental and the state's purpose or effect must be strictly reviewed. Thus, when the state statute provided that violations of the prohibitory laws, revenue acts, embezzlement, or political offenses, though within the same class of felonies, would not be punished in the same manner as larceny, the offenses for which Skinner was prosecuted, the Court used an equal protection analysis to determine if the statute was treating all persons similarly situated in a similar manner.

The Court pointed out the inequalities in the Oklahoma Act by writing that both grand larceny and embezzlement are felonies and the nature of the two crimes are the same, but the two offenses are not punished in the same manner by the Oklahoma statute. Because the right to procreate is held to be fundamental the Court strictly reviewed the classification (as applied to all persons affected by the Act). The decision of the Court, on an Equal Protection Clause rationale, was based upon the law being applied to those who had committed the same quality of offenses being treated differently. The sterilization of those who had thrice committed grand larceny with immunity for those who were embezzlers, also a felony of a similar type,[28] was described as "unmistakable" discrimination.

The foregoing explanation of the Court's majority opinion is difficult to understand without an awareness of the substantive concepts involved. The assigned class readings and law class discussion will give the student sufficient background to understand the Court's opinion. It is, therefore, rather obvious that significant preparation for class participation is necessary.

Justice Douglas's opinion of the Court is the majority opinion because, as previously described, five or more members of the Court agreed upon both how the case should be decided and the reason the Court should decide the case as it did. The majority opinion is that which is the binding precedent. A precedent is the rule of law that the Court applies to the facts of the case that are necessary for decision. Thus, when one analyzes a case it is necessary to decide what facts are necessary for the court to consider in its deliberations for decision purposes.

Additional comment, for background purposes, will be offered as "comment" subsequent to the sample brief that follows.

Sample Brief

Skinner v. Oklahoma, p. 182 (1942).

Relevant Facts: This case requires the Supreme Court to determine the constitutionality of Oklahoma's Habitual Criminal Sterilization Act that was applied to the petitioner, Skinner, by the Oklahoma Court. The Act defines a "habitual criminal" as a person who, having been convicted two or more times for felonies involving moral turpitude in either Oklahoma or another state and thereafter is convicted of such a felony in Oklahoma and sentenced to prison. The Act then provides authority for the attorney general (AG) to institute a proceeding in the Oklahoma courts for a judgment that the habitual criminal is to be rendered sexually sterile. The statute provides that the judicial review in the action brought by the AG will be limited to whether the sterilization can occur without detriment to the defendant's general health. The jury found that the sterilization could be conducted without detriment to defendant's health, and the defendant was not given an opportunity to be heard on the issue concerning whether he could be the potential parent of socially undesirable offspring. The Court recognized that appellant contended that the Act was violative of the Eighth Amendment's prohibition of cruel and unusual punishment and the Fourteenth Amendment (presumably the Due Process Clause); however, the Court asserted it "passed those points without intimating an opinion on them" to write to the failure of the Act to meet the requirements of the Equal Protection Clause of the Fourteenth Amendment. The Equal Protection Clause basis for the Court's decision rests upon the different treatment of defendants charged with embezzlement rather than larceny, i.e., those charged with embezzlement, a felony just as larceny and the same quality of offense, are not subject to sterilization.

Issue:[29] Whether a state statute that requires that persons who have been convicted thrice for crimes involving moral turpitude may be rendered sterile if there is a judicial finding that the procedure would not injure the general health of the defendant, yet excepting embezzlement, tax evasion and political offenses, is a violation of the Equal Protection Clause of the Fourteenth Amendment? Yes.

Rationale:

1. Where the nature of the two crimes, larceny and embezzlement, is, as the Court asserts, "intrinsically the same," but are not punishable in the same manner, persons similarly situated are not being treated in a similar manner. The Oklahoma legislation "runs afoul" the Equal Protection Clause of the Fourteenth Amendment that provides that states shall not "deny to any person within its jurisdiction the equal protection of the laws."
2. The Court's opinion notes that the states are generally given deference in applying the Equal Protection Clause; however, here the legislation involves "one of the basic civil rights of man," i.e., marriage and procreation, held to be fundamental to the very "existence and survival of the race."
3. The Court then noted that the "basic liberty" to change the standard of review from deference to be given to the state to "strict scru-

tiny" of the government's statute occurs when government regulation infringes upon a fundamental right, here the right to procreate. The opinion then asserts that: "when the law lays an unequal hand on those who have committed intrinsically the same quality of offense and sterilizes one and not the other it has made as invidious discrimination as if it had selected a particular race or nationality for oppressive treatment."

4. Oklahoma made no attempt to show that one committing larceny had biologically different inheritable traits from one who commits embezzlement. Thus, the state failed to justify the different treatment for those committing the two offenses.[30]

Precedent: A state statute that requires that persons who have been convicted thrice for crimes involving moral turpitude may be rendered sterile if there is a judicial finding that the procedure would not injure the general health of the defendant, yet excepting crimes that are intrinsically the same from the sterilization requirement, is a violation of the Equal Protection Clause of the Fourteenth Amendment.[31]

Concurrence: Chief Justice Stone's concurring opinion agrees that the state statute is unconstitutional but would use the Due Process Clause of the Fourteenth Amendment as the reason for the holding. He wrote that:

> "[T]he most elementary notions of due process would seem to require [the State] to take appropriate steps to safeguard the liberty of the individual by affording him, before he is condemned to irreparable injury in his person, some opportunity to show that he is without such inheritable tendencies. The state is ... required to reach its objective by a reasonable and just procedure adequate to safeguard rights of the individual which concededly the Constitution protects."[32]

The separate concurring opinion of Justice Jackson is omitted.

Thus, the concurrence of Chief Justice Stone, quoted above, offers a rationale for his decision based on procedural due process rather than, as the opinion of the Skinner Court, the Equal Protection Clause. The analysis, i.e., "briefing" of an abstract in a casebook for class purposes, is that which the law student must accomplish individually. The first "brief" prepared by the beginning law student will be long and difficult. Take heart! The process becomes easier with experience. Note, however, one does not obtain the necessary experience by using "cans" (commercial renditions of a brief prepared for sale to the student, akin to CliffNotes) or notes on briefs prepared by law students in previous years. The beginning law student should perform his or her work independently of study aids and treatises to the maximum extent possible. The writers of this material are cognizant that some study aids, especially treatises (commonly called "Hornbooks") are very helpful in offering an explanation of the case and giving the "big picture" concerning the subject matter treated by the case or cases covered in class. We strongly suggest that the student attempt to analyze the case first, ascertaining the legal issue or issues, and try to understand what the Court held concerning the issues posed, as well as the rationale asserted by the Court for the decision, before using study aids. Study aids are excellent if a suitable quality aid is used to reinforce the learning process, not to bypass learning to analyze the case. The student who does not take the opportunity to learn to analyze cases during the first year of law school will find it very difficult to improve the ability to analyze in the second and third years of the law school experience.

Sample Torts Case

The second selected case is from the area of law called, "torts." Torts is a standard first semester, first year required course in almost all American law schools. The word tort is derived from a Latin word tortus and a French word tort. In Latin tortus means, "twisted," and in

French tort means, "injury or wrong." The classic definition of a tort is as follows: "A tort is a civil wrong, other than a breach of contract, for which the law provides a remedy."[33] In its simplest form, this fundamental area of the law deals with a lawsuit brought in a civil court by one person, the plaintiff, against another person, the defendant, for an alleged harm suffered by the plaintiff and caused by the defendant.

A successful lawsuit allows a plaintiff to recover money damages for the personal harm suffered by the plaintiff. From the first torts class, the student learns to distinguish a tort from a crime. A crime is an offense against the state's criminal law and is punished by fine or imprisonment. A tort is a harm that allows an injured person to receive damages. Sometimes, but by no means always, the same facts give rise to both a criminal case and a tort case. For example, in a barroom brawl, a defendant may have committed a criminal act and the state may seek a criminal penalty. But, even with a successful prosecution, putting the defendant in jail does nothing to help a plaintiff who was injured by the defendant's conduct. The tort suit by the plaintiff will enable him or her to seek damage for the wrong suffered. Note that a "civil" wrong was suffered and a personal remedy is found in a "civil suit"—our tort action.

The fact patterns giving rise to civil wrongs are endless in their variety. Nevertheless, there are three general categories of tort actions: "intentional" torts, "negligent" torts, and "strict liability" torts. In an intentional tort, the defendant is alleged to have committed an act "with knowledge, or substantial certainty" that the act would cause harmful or offensive contact to the plaintiff. In a negligent tort, the defendant's conduct fell below that of a reasonable prudent person and caused injury to the plaintiff. Notice that recovery in either an intentional tort case or a negligent tort is based on the fault of the defendant. This is called fault-based liability. An example of a "strict liability" tort is where the defendant engages in an activity that is ultra-hazardous, (example: blasting at a construction site) and causes the plaintiff harm even though there was no negligence or carelessness; in a strict liability case, the defendant pays for any damage without regard to fault.

The following tort case selected for analysis and briefing comes from the area of intentional torts.

Fisher v. Carrousel Motor Hotel, Inc.

Supreme Court of Texas, 1967
424 S.W.2d 627.

> [Action for assault and battery. Plaintiff, a mathematician employed by NASA was attending a professional conference on telemetry equipment at defendant's hotel. The meeting included a buffet luncheon. As plaintiff was standing in line with others, he was approached by one of defendant's employees who snatched the plate from his hand, and shouted that a "Negro could not be served in the club." Plaintiff was not actually touched and was in no apprehension of physical injury; but he was highly embarrassed and hurt by the conduct in the presence of his associates. The jury returned a verdict of $400 actual damages for his humiliation and indignity, and $500 exemplary (punitive) damages in addition. The trial court set aside the verdict and gave judgment for the defendants notwithstanding the verdict. This was affirmed by the Court of Appeals. Plaintiff appealed to the Supreme Court.]
>
> GREENHILL, JUSTICE *** Under the facts of this case, we have no difficulty in holding that the intentional grabbing of plaintiff's plate constituted a battery. The intentional snatching of an object from one's hand is as clearly an offensive invasion of his person as would be an actual contact with the body. "To constitute an assault and battery, it is not necessary to touch the plaintiff's body or even his clothing; knocking or snatching anything from plaintiff's body or even touching anything connected with his person, when done in an offensive manner, is sufficient." Morgan v. Loyacomo, 190 Miss. 656, 1 So.2d 510 (1941).

Such holding is not unique to the jurisprudence of this State. In S.H. Kress & Co. v. Brashier, 50 S.W.2d 922 (TexCiv. App.1932, no writ), the defendant was held to have committed "an assault or trespass upon the person" by snatching a book from the plaintiff's hand. The jury findings in that case were that the defendant "dispossessed plaintiff of the book" and caused her to suffer "humiliation and indignity."

The rationale for holding an offensive contact with such an object to be a battery is explained in 1 Restatement (Second) of Torts § 18 (Comment p. 31) as follows:

"Since the essence of the plaintiff's grievance consists in the offense to the dignity involved in the unpermitted and intentional invasion of the inviolability of his person and not in any physical harm done to his body, it is not necessary that the plaintiff's actual body be disturbed. Unpermitted and intentional contacts with anything so connected with the body as to be customarily regarded as part of the other's person and therefore as partaking of its inviolability is actionable as an offensive contact with his person. There are some things such as clothing or a cane or, indeed, anything directly grasped by the hand which are so intimately connected with one's body as to be universally regarded as part of the person."

We hold, therefore, that the forceful dispossession of plaintiff Fisher's plate in an offensive manner was sufficient to constitute a battery, and the trial court erred in granting judgment notwithstanding the verdict on the issue of actual damages. * * *

Damages for mental suffering are recoverable without the necessity for showing actual physical injury in a case of willful battery because the basis of that action is the unpermitted and intentional invasion of the plaintiff's person and not the actual harm done to the plaintiff's body. Restatement (Second) of Torts § 18. Personal indignity is the essence of an action for battery; and consequently the defendant is liable not only for contacts which do actual physical harm but also for those which are offensive and insulting. [Cc]. We hold, therefore, that plaintiff was entitled to actual damages

> for mental suffering due to the willful battery, even in the absence of any physical injury. [The court then held that the defendant corporation was liable for the tort of its employee.]
>
> The judgments of the courts below are reversed, and judgment is here rendered for the plaintiff for $900 with interest from the date of the trial court's judgment, and costs of this suit. [34]

The Fisher case is a fascinating one that occurred in the civil-rights era at a time of great racial tension in the United States. The Supreme Court of Texas was faced with a case of flagrant racism, but where no physical harm had resulted. The Court used the ancient intentional tort of "battery" to provide relief. The old common law inherited from England defined the "least touching of another in anger" as a battery. Allowing the injured or offended plaintiff to sue for damages was a way to provide a remedy to the plaintiff. Without such a remedy a plaintiff might seek redress, which might cause further breach of the peace.

A sample brief of the Fisher case is followed by a short commentary.

Sample Brief

Fisher v. Carrousel Motor Hotel, Supreme Court of Texas p.35 (1967)

Relevant Facts: Plaintiff was an African-American mathematician employed by NASA. Plaintiff was attending, as a part of his professional obligation, a conference on telemetry equipment; the conference was held in defendant's hotel. After the morning session, it is reported that those attending the conference, about twenty-five to thirty persons, went to the hotel restaurant for a buffet-line lunch. Plaintiff was standing in the buffet line with his plate in his hand when the restaurant manager grabbed the plate from him, shouting that "a negro could not be served." There was no allegation that the manager physically touched the plaintiff's body.

The Issue: Can the "touching" element of the tort of battery be met if the physical contact is not with the body but instead with items closely connected with the plaintiff's person?

The Procedural Posture of the Case. After a jury verdict for the plaintiff, the trial judge granted a "judgment notwithstanding the verdict" "JNOV" setting aside the jury's verdict and entering a decision for the defendant hotel. The appellate court affirmed the action of the trial judge. The Texas Supreme Court reversed the appellate court; it had "no difficulty in holding that the grabbing of the plaintiff's plate constituted a battery."

Rationale: The Texas Supreme Court, in reversing the lower courts and finding for the plaintiff, following a number of other, older cases that extended the element of "touching" required in a tort of battery to include items that are so closely associated with the body that they amount to an invasion of bodily integrity.

Commentary: This simple case is an example of an appellate court setting a precedent for the lower courts of its state. It authorizes expansion of battery suits to cover egregious conduct that is not an actual physical touching, but contact with something that is so intimately associated with the body as to amount to sufficient "touching" to satisfy the legal requirements for a tort of battery. Why allow this conduct—which caused no physical harm at all and did not even actually "touch" the body—to be sufficient for monetary damages? Is the court concerned only about preventing breach of the peace? Or, more broadly, is it concerned with protecting the intrinsic dignity of all citizens, regardless of race, from outrageous public insult? These questions will be discussed at length in class. Variations on the Fisher fact pattern will be posed to try to draw the line between touching and non-touching. For example, the Prosser casebook authors ask hypothetically, "What if the manager merely shouted, Get out, we don't serve negroes here!" Why did the plaintiff need to sue for a battery at all? Why not sue for the modern tort of "Intentional Infliction of Emotional Harm?" The extraordinary and endless variety of fact patterns that can cause harm to individuals, and for which recovery is sought in our civil courts, might be thought of as a study of the evolution of a civilized society itself. Through the centuries courts have attempted to maintain social harmony and avoid vigilante justice. We guarantee your torts course will be fascinating, provocative, and immerse you in a far better understanding of the critical role that our courts and our laws play in maintaining a civilized law-abiding society.

Class Preparation

One could sum up relevant class preparation advice to a first year law student quickly. It is necessary to prepare for each class if the student expects to both enjoy the class experience and follow the discussion satisfactorily. The question the student must answer is what type of activity or activities best serves to prepare for class.

Not all students prepare for class in the same manner. Obviously, advice concerning class preparation must be offered generally and the student must settle upon the method or methods most effective for him or her. The general suggestions that follow are offered to give the law student the benefit of considering class preparation methods that are generally recognized as helpful and—after the experience of law school, as both students and professors—the authors offer for student consideration.

First, we should consider study habits generally. Law students should not rely upon the "cram" approach some of them found satisfactory in undergraduate school. There is too much material in law school to allow one to use methods that the student found satisfactory in undergraduate school courses, unless the student studied diligently with effective study methods prior to law school. In fact, even effective study methods prior to law school may require modification to be effective in law school. Importantly, cramming is generally accompanied by "dumping"; that is, the release of crammed information from short-term memory and the failure to truly learn the concept. This type of approach is undesirable, as law studies prepare the student for the bar exam and legal practice—endeavors that demand fluency in legal concepts and application.

Entering law students in ABA approved law schools have been determined to be qualified to seek a legal education by the entrance requirements of the law school to which they are admitted. Some law students, however, are more successful than their colleagues due to the manner in which they approach the requisites for success. The comments that follow will offer suggestions for entering law students who are either searching for the best methods for success in law school or those who recognize that they should be willing to consider refining the methods for learning that were used in undergraduate school to improve their academic performance.

Many law professors and practicing lawyers agree that the first year of the law school curriculum is truly the most important. In the first year, one learns new concepts and processes that will aid them for the rest of their lives should they remain a part of the legal profession. A student's academic reputation among peers is usually cemented in the first semester, if not the first year. Access to extra curricular endeavors, such as law review, is generally based on early academic success. Furthermore, summer employment and clerkship opportunities generally will look to the law student's performance during the first year, thus the first year law student should make every effort to excel.

Develop A Learning Methodology That Is Best For You

The entering law student must develop a learning and study methodology that is both effective and best for the individual. The methodology should develop a broad plan that addresses all of the courses that must be negotiated during the semester. The plan should then be specifically designed to recognize the differences in the material offered in each course. Most importantly, the learning plan should consider how the student will approach the learning process in each course. Some courses require more time than others, and some are more difficult. Thus, consciously arrange a study schedule that provides time for each course and subsequently, vary that plan as you become more familiar with each course during the semester. Study the professor's syllabus and meet with the professor to refine your understanding of how to properly plan in order to master the material in each course.[35] Many students avoid meeting with their professors and attempt to remain as anonymous as possible in class. Such an approach is a gross mistake. Professors have office hours. Make an appointment to meet with your professor each semester to obtain an insight concerning how you should prepare for the course. Students who use even one aspect of formulating a plan to negotiate the law school curriculum, such as goal setting, tend to outperform students who do not set goals.

Recognize The Expectations of The Professor

Professors in law school generally expect much effective effort from the students in their classes. Whereas students have a right to expect competence and dedication from their professors, that right is a two-way street. The professor has the right to expect competence and dedication from each student in the class. Students should take an active role in class, rather than merely passively receiving information. Experience in teaching law school indicates that the most effective law students are those who actively participate in the study of the subject matter required for each law school course. Thus, the entering law student should take every course seriously and not be passive in class, merely reading, preparing for class, and attempting to absorb the material discussed without participating in the discussion. Students should prepare the assigned material for each class and treat class as a means to reinforce that which was learned from out-of-class preparation. If one does not feel reinforced in class after preparing the material assigned for the class in question, they should consider preparing differently prior to attending subsequent classes.

The student should feel free to ask relevant questions and, most certainly, express oneself adequately in answering questions. The student will find it appropriate to meet with the professor during office hours for additional explanations not relevant to the material and to explain aspects of the assigned material that the class followed but the individual student did not.

Law Students Should Take Responsibility for Their Individual Preparation and Learning

Law students must take responsibility for their own preparation and learning. The professor for each course can aid the law student both in and out of class if the student takes responsibility to master the material themselves. In essence, the learning that will be most valuable and meaningful to the law students will come from their own initiative. Do not expect the professor to make you learn or entertain you while doing his or her job. Each class is an opportunity to learn both new material and obtain the discipline necessary to absorb that material. There is no way that one can absorb and retain all that we hear and read in both preparing for and participating in numerous classes each day. Law students must take notes, not in an attempt to make a verbatim record of that which the professor utters, but to memorialize notes of relevant thoughts and concepts that will refresh one's memory for both reflection and examination purposes. A class outline should be prepared for each class from day one of the classroom experience. The outline should contain the notes and briefs, or important excerpts therefrom, that the student has prepared for purposes of attending the class and be embellished upon by the concepts and comments made in class that will aid in refreshing the student's memory. A course outline that is a work-in-progress throughout the semester, used for both class preparation and for examination review purposes, should be created by the student for each class. The depth of material necessary for an adequate course outline can be explained by recognition that law examinations are generally administered only at the end of the semester for each subject. A sample examination is included at the end of these text materials. [36]

The First Year of the Law School Curriculum Will Require The Law Student To Acquire and Use a Great Deal of Knowledge

Unfortunately, some law students find it more difficult to convey knowledge gained from preparation in both class and on examinations than is the case with some of their colleagues. Law school examinations require the student to demonstrate skills in applying knowledge gained to new, or analogous, situations as well as those that were specifically discussed or studied. Acquiring new skills requires one to practice those skills. Practicing new skills and using new knowledge requires that one learn to convey that new knowledge to others through both oral explanation and the written word. The law student learns from both the briefing and outlining activity. The briefs and outline will, as mentioned earlier, be both difficult to write and longer at first than will be true after experience is gained. The experience gained by doing one's own work is extremely important to both mastering the materials and gaining the confidence necessary to succeed in both law school and subsequent law practice.

Oral explanation and discussion are excellent ways to further understand the materials studied and to learn to convey that material to others. Class discussion is one of the first areas of emphasis that the law student should concentrate upon. If one can discuss the material in class through both responding to questions from the professor and asking relevant questions, it is possible to learn more about the material and to inform the professor of the student's interest in the learning process. Such also contributes to the learning process of your classmates and builds relationships that will aid you throughout your professional life. The classroom experience is one of the most important aspects of legal education.

Law school is expensive. The law student should attend every class possible, even those classes for which the student feels unprepared. Professors would much prefer that students attend class and gain as much as possible from attending than refraining from attending because time did not allow appropriate preparation.

Selection of Elective Courses

The first year curriculum in most law schools consists of required courses. However, during the second year students can select many, if not most, of the courses they take from a long list of elective courses and seminars. The third year at most schools consists of totally elective courses, seminars, skills courses, and externships. How does a student go about selecting courses from the elective list?

1. Student Interest Areas: What areas interested you most in your first year courses? If contracts was fascinating, think about electives in the business and corporations area. If it was torts that turned you on, litigation courses such as evidence, federal courts, trial advocacy, and skills courses should be options. You have the chance, in a broad sense, to prepare generally for your ultimate practice areas.
2. The Bar Exam: What areas are tested in your state's bar examination? One should take electives in all subject areas of the bar examination which are not covered in the required curriculum. The subjects on the bar exam will be available from the law school assistant dean of student affairs and by direct contact with the applicable state bar association.

3. Basic Preparation For Practice: Regardless of the possible areas of future practice that interest you, you need a broad, general exposure to the major areas of practice because you really don't know where you will end up. For example, you may think that a corporate or business practice is not for you, but regardless of your specialty, all lawyers must have a basic understanding of how business operates under our laws. Therefore, take a basic corporations course. Even if you aren't interested in trial work, every lawyer must know how trials operate, so take a basic evidence course. The world is getting smaller; take a good international or comparative law course. Basic courses in tax, administrative law, and wills and trusts are helpful to all lawyers. One or more third year elective skills courses in such areas as negotiations, counseling, alternative dispute resolution, trial practice, and appellate practice are helpful. A specialty seminar that requires a well-researched original paper will improve your writing skills and expand the depth of knowledge you have in an interest area.
4. Seek Advice: Most law schools provide advisors or student advising programs to aid you in elective course selections. Seek out such advice.

Law Students Must Adequately Develop and Continue to Improve Their Writing Skills

One of the most important aspects of communicating in both law school and law practice is the ability to properly convey one's thoughts through writing. Many entering law students are very bright but have not developed their writing skills adequately upon entering law school to realize their full potential. Those law students who write well upon entry to law school should strive to write even better. If, however, one does not convey their thoughts through writing adequately to be understood they should concentrate on improving that ability prior to taking examinations. Both excellent writers and those who would like to become excellent writers should write out their briefs during the course of the semester in preparing for class, whether such is done by computer or handwritten. Preparing for class and properly organizing notes and briefs daily to develop course outlines will tend to improve writing ability as well as an understanding of the subject matter studied.

Briefing Cases

One could first ask why law students are required to brief cases for classes. The simple answer to the question could be recognized as merely to avoid being embarrassed by not being in a position to respond when called upon in class to offer an analysis of a case assigned for the particular class in question. While such an answer is obviously a good reason, there are many other good reasons as well. First, as previously mentioned, we must recognize that lawyers are problem solvers. The case which you will brief relates to a problem or problems which are appropriate for judicial determination.[37] Hence, when a case is read for purposes of briefing the reader is seeking an understanding of the problem that the court is solving (the legal issues for decision), the manner in which the problem is solved, and the reason (or rationale) for the Court's decision. As previously noted in discussion of the Skinner case,[38] one must first determine the facts which the court considered as necessary to decide the legal issue or issues which were necessary to establish the basis for the problem itself. The legal issue or issues are determined by the facts which the court considers necessary for purposes of decision. Thus, in essence, the issue or issues in a case are merely those questions which the court must answer to decide the case. The reasoning for the court's decision, the rationale for the decision, is that which is offered by the court for lawyers to determine why the court decided the case as it did. Therefore, when a majority of the justices of an appellate court decide the case in the same manner and for the same reasons the appellate court has established a binding precedent for the judicial district or geographical area for which the court has appellate responsibility. Trial courts do not decide precedents, trial courts follow binding precedents.

To reiterate, an issue is defined as the legal question that the court must decide to decide the case. The legal issue is determined by the facts which the court must consider in order to decide the case. The reasoning, or rationale, is merely the reason which the court used for purposes of deciding the case. In the legal culture of the United States the courts follow Stare Decisis.[39] The precedent of a case is the legal rule which the court applies to the facts which are necessary for decision in the case before it. The doctrine of Stare Decisis provides that the binding precedent of a case controls not only the outcome of that particular case, but also other cases within the appellate jurisdiction in question which have facts necessary for decision closely analogous to the case decided and the legal rule applied to those closely analogous facts is the same.[40]

Use of Student Study Groups

Many law students use study groups at some time during the law school experience. If, and only if, the group is composed of serious and competent students the group can be helpful. Avoid selecting or joining a group which spends most of its time as an opportunity to socialize to the detriment of study. Socialization is important; however, expect a study group to study by discussing the materials for which the session was planned. Study of the materials to be discussed in the study group should occur on an individual basis before the group convenes. The use of a study group to write one's class outline after the materials have been individually prepared can constitute a good review of the material and reinforce a prior review of the material. Study group discussion can also reinforce both the student's prior preparation and class coverage. One should avoid the waste of valuable time that can occur with one or more colleagues that are unprepared.

Preparing Course Outlines with Personal Notes, Briefs, Commercial Outlines, and Textbooks

The foundation for course outlines begins with the student's prepared briefs and class notes from the class where the cases briefed were discussed. One could, after experiencing the "learning-by-briefing" use a relevant textbook (preferably one suggested by the professor with responsibility for the course in question) to determine the information that should be written into the class outline to aid in reviewing the course material for examination. The first course outlines, just as the first case "briefs" written by the student, will be much longer than those prepared for courses after the first semester. The outline will diminish in length, while improving as a study aid, with experience as the student progresses through law school. The student should commence compilation of an outline for each course as quickly as possible after the semester begins, and such should be a work in progress throughout each semester.

The earlier in the semester one begins his outline of materials in each course the better. In all events, the student should not wait until study for the examination formally begins. Early and consistent outline preparation throughout the semester is, as a matter of fact, studying for the examination and will reduce much of the nervousness that occurs in preparation for the final exam. Most law school courses for which exams are applicable (seminars are considered to be courses in which the grade is primarily determined by student preparation of a written research paper) will offer only one exam at the end of the semester or quarter.

The course outline is an excellent means of preparing for the exam on a continuous basis. Students who purchase a course outline either commercially or from an upper class law student do not receive the learning experience that occurs from compiling their own outlines. There is an obvious benefit when the student creates organized study materials from classes with the professor during the applicable time-frame. Professors change both materials and teaching techniques. The best materials for study purposes are those that the student prepares for the class in question. In all events, the course outline should contain the information developed during class preparation and participation in sufficient detail to refresh the student's memory when preparing for the final examination.

Developing the Ability to State Legal Issues in the Context of the Facts Presented in the Case Before the Court

This topic was first offered in the materials following the sample cases and comments to allow the reader to understand a case abstract and sample brief.[41] The concept of stating the legal issue, or issues, in the context of the facts that the court must consider in deciding the issue is again stressed here for several reasons. First, if the student will read the case abstract carefully and determine the issues and necessary facts to be considered sufficiently to develop the issue on a fact-contextual basis, the student will understand the reasoning offered by the court and the rule of law (statute or binding precedent) which the court applied. Second, a contextual issue can be stated in a declarative manner to understand the scope of the precedent for future application to other appropriate cases.

The student should recognize that the contention, or contentions, of the party or parties appealing the decision of the lower court (the appellant or appellants) will generally be that which the court is required to decide, and thus, the issue that will determine how the case will be decided. The foregoing statement is not true, however, when the court below or the court in which the appeal is filed has no power to decide the case. In such a case, the appellate court will recognize it has no jurisdiction, i.e., no power to decide the case and dismiss it without considering the contentions of the parties.

Preparing for Examinations

Exam preparation commences at the time the student prepares for the first class. One should memorialize the results of one's study of the assigned materials. Placing the material in an organized manner by class is generally recognized as preferable because that is the manner in which one prepares. Periodically, as often as possible given the nature of the work-load in law school, one should consolidate briefs, notes from class, and other relevant material into an outline for exam preparation in a cohesive compilation. In all events, use one's own, personally developed outline for examination preparation. A sample law school examination is included with these materials as Appendix C. Review of the exam will reveal the importance of student class preparation and review materials assigned for class. Law examinations generally provide the student with an opportunity to utilize materials studied during the semester. An outline of materials covered during the semester will refresh the student's memory and enhance the quality of responses to exam questions.

Review of Examination Results

Professors in ABA approved law schools retain the graded examination response papers for one year after the exam period is complete. The student can profit from reviewing the exam response submitted in responses to the exam questions. We suggest that you inquire concerning the professors exam review procedure and take advantage of the opportunity to review your exam submission. Exam review will provide a basis to review how questions were answered and improve the next submission. Do not, however, ask for a grade review or expect such unless the grading mistake is obvious from your review, e.g., where the addition or subtraction on the paper is evidence of the error. Professors in ABA approved schools carefully grade the exams that they write and mistakes occur very infrequently. Obviously, however, professors are human and where quantifiable mistakes have been made such should be brought to the professor's attention.

Success in Taking the Bar Exam

You have completed law school successfully. You are ready to start practice. But wait, there is this obstacle called the bar examination. You may not like it, but it commands your respectful attention! Too many law students take this last hurdle too lightly. Do not ignore the necessity of preparing vigorously for your last, and most meaningful, pre-practice examination to allow you to become a lawyer.

In the four- to eight-week period between your graduation and the bar examination the problems of life will attempt to intrude on your critical preparation time. Some students decide to commence married life, some make a major move to another city, some want to take that last holiday, and some commence full-time employment too quickly. But that prime four- to eight-week period is your only chance to prepare for a rigorous and exhausting two- or three-day bar examination that covers your three or four year law school experience. Most law school graduates who fail the bar examination do so because they didn't take the time to prepare properly. Some law schools are now offering a "not for credit" course in the last semester to help students get ready. If you have this option, take it. In any event, take a good bar review course prior to the examination. Take that course seriously and study, full-time, while taking it. Many good lawyers have survived flunking the bar the first time, but you do not want to have that experience. You waste time, money and self-esteem. It simply is not worth the risk.

Transitioning from Law School to Practice

The American higher education system provides the best legal training in the world. Four years of undergraduate experience, coupled with three additional years of intensive legal training produces highly qualified people. This begs the question, qualified for what? Unfortunately, law school does not train people to be successful lawyers. Admittedly, a law school graduate who passes the bar has a number of very important skills. A young lawyer probably knows more "black letter" law than most seasoned practitioners. Most law students understand how the American legal system works. They are trained to find the law, to analyze it and to predict an outcome, based on the facts presented. Some students, those who participate in trial advocacy programs, probably have the rudimentary skills necessary to try a simple case in court. But law school does not do a good job of teaching students to be successful lawyers, particularly in the highly competitive world of private practice. The materials that follow will discuss some fairly obvious and not so obvious matters the new graduate should consider to successfully transition from the study of law to the practice of law. We turn our attention first to the types of jobs available and the reality of starting pay.

Jobs and Pay

Statistics show that about 56.5 percent of recent graduates will enter private practice as a first job out of law school.[43] Business and industry employ the next largest segment of young lawyers, 14.1 percent. About 10.7 percent of graduates work in government, not including judicial clerkships.[42] And, 9.8 percent of graduates work in judicial clerkships. The public interest sector (public defender's office and non-profit advocacy groups) employ 5.8 percent of new graduates. The academic world employs 1.8 percent of graduates. The military accounts for 1 percent of new jobs for graduates.

A recent Wall Street Journal article reports that "[a] law degree isn't necessarily a license to print money today."[44] A slack in demand appears to be the problem. "Tort reform" in some states has curbed the personal injury and medical malpractice sectors of the legal practice. And, until recently, a booming stock market has caused security cases to decline in frequency. Consumer and employment arbitration have caused fewer cases to be filed and smaller recoveries to be had. Meanwhile, law schools have surged, both in the number of schools and the number of graduates. The net result is that more lawyers are working for less pay.

Although big firm salaries in large cities reported starting salaries of up to $160,000 in 2007, only the best students from top schools are employed by such firms. Indeed, a common complaint at most law schools is that only the highest ranking students have meaningful choices at graduation. Those graduating at the bottom of the class frequently graduate with fewer employment prospects.

Salary statistics are somewhat dubious, as students who do well have a greater tendency to respond to surveys than those who do not. Salaries for students graduating in 2007 averaged in the sixty-thousand-dollar range. Thus half of all graduates earned less and half earned more. Private practice skews the salary figures upward. Government, judicial clerkships, and public interest employment all reported national median incomes of fifty thousand dollars or less. Unfortunately, new lawyers who do land a top job at a large firm will not see much of a pay increase in the first several years of practice. To afford the "overpaid" new lawyers, firms have a tendency to underpay associates as they progress to partnership. It is not uncommon to find only a few thousand dollars difference in pay between starting lawyers and lawyers with five to six years of experience. Wage compression, which is a function of overpaying young lawyers, is a necessary evil to attract the brightest and best.

The late 2008 economy presented the worst hiring environment in recent memory. Fewer students acquired jobs before graduation. Although the data is still anecdotal at this point, career services departments reported fewer job opportunities for 2009 graduates. Not surprisingly, students who were offered jobs before the economic collapse are accepting less pay than promised or anticipated because of salary renegotiations. The credit crunch has curtailed transactional work, and business lawyers are struggling, which translates to fewer new hires in corporate departments of firms and corporations. Now, more than ever, law students need to work harder and smarter if they are to be successful in obtaining employment and keeping it. Nevertheless, there are large segments of our population that are substantially underserved by the legal profession. This is caused by a mal-distribution of legal talent.

The training offered in law schools is as diverse as the practice of law. There is no single roadmap to success. However, specific career paths do require certain specialized training. The discussion that follows will offer guidance on course selection and desirable extracurricular activities.

Class Selection

Does this sentiment sound familiar? "I only want to take classes that I like and can do well in." From an undergraduate perspective, this is a perfectly normal and realistic perspective. The fact is that many college students seek out "crib" classes in an effort to pad the UGPA to maximize post-graduate opportunities. However, this strategy is generally not effective in law school if the aim is to pass the bar exam and obtain worthy employment.

In the first year of law school, as previously discussed, the curriculum is generally inflexible. The student takes a standard fare of required courses that include contracts, torts, property, civil procedure, criminal law, and legal research and writing, among other classes. The law student can make an intelligent choice in areas of law to pursue after experience gained in law school. The second year of training provides greater flexibility, but may still require certain required courses, including constitutional law, business associations, evidence, and coursework in the Uniform Commercial Code (the sale of goods, negotiable instruments and commercial paper). The curriculum permits a handful of elective courses in the second year of training. There is generally only one other required course—professional responsibility (a course that teaches the ethics of lawyering). Students are permitted to take a variety of elective courses in areas of personal interest and aptitude. There are at least two reasons that course selection matters. First, every budding lawyer has the option of sitting for a bar examination at the completion of law school. Successful completion of the bar exam is a necessary prerequisite to licensure as a practicing lawyer. The bar exam is a rigorous two or three day test, depending on the jurisdiction, that requires mastery of a number of disciplines and subject matter. Avoiding undesirable subject matter in law school that is tested on the bar has obvious pitfalls. Therefore—as has been previously mentioned but important enough to emphasize—students are encouraged to take classes that are treated on the bar. Second, prospective employers demand at least some law school training in their areas of specialty. The following discussion offers suggestions regarding the courses one should consider to successfully navigate the bar exam and obtain desirable employment.

The Bar Exam[45]

If graduation from law school is one of the best days in a person's life, then surely the days that follow—preparing for and taking the bar exam—qualify as some of the worst. The bar exam is actually comprised of a number of tests (depending on the jurisdiction). Graduating students spend about sixty to ninety grueling days following graduation studying for the bar exam. The bar examination is typically offered twice per year, in the last weeks in July and February. A separate test on legal ethics is offered at various times during a student's second and third year of study. Most jurisdictions require a student to pass both tests as a condition of licensure. The bar exam ranks as one of the toughest professional tests in the country.

One full day of the examination consists of a two-hundred-question multiple-choice test that is identical for all law students nationwide. This test is known as the Multistate Bar Examination ("MBE"). The MBE is written by the National Conference of Bar Examiners. It tests proficiency in the following areas: contracts, torts, real property, constitutional law, criminal law, criminal procedure, and evidence. There was a time when each of these courses was required at every law school. However, some schools do not require constitutional law or evidence as part of their core curriculum. The MBE is divided into two three-hour sessions. It tests fundamental legal principles, as opposed to state-specific knowledge of statutes and case law. Students analyze fact patterns presented in the questions and are required to choose the best answer from among four choices. General law school training, coupled with the courses in the subject matter described above, is a must for success on the MBE.

All states require a second day of testing, and in some states, a third day of testing is required. Almost half of the states offer a uniform essay test known as the Multistate Essay Exam ("MEE"). Non-participating states offer their own state-specific essay questions. The MEE is a collection of up to nine thirty-minute essays. Most jurisdictions select six of the nine questions. The questions are developed from the following list of twelve topics, only some of which are required courses in most law schools: business associations, conflict of laws, constitutional law, contracts, criminal law and procedure, evidence, family law, federal civil procedure, real property, torts, trusts and estates, and the Uniform Commercial Code. A strong background in each of these subjects is desirable for this part of the bar.

Over half of US jurisdictions also require a test known as the Multistate Performance Test ("MPT"). The MPT consists of two ninety-minute skills questions covering factual analysis, legal analysis, resolving ethical dilemmas, problem solving, communication, and organizing and managing lawyer tasks. The MPT requires applicants to:

> "(1) sort detailed factual materials and separate relevant from irrelevant facts; (2) analyze statutory, case, and administrative materials for relevant principles of law; (3) apply the relevant law to the relevant facts in a manner likely to resolve a client's problem; (4) identify and resolve ethical dilemmas, when present; (5) communicate effectively in writing; (6) complete a lawyering task within time constraints."[46]

The exam will usually ask the test-taker to complete:

> "a memorandum to a supervising attorney; a letter to a client; a persuasive memorandum or brief; a statement of facts; a contract provision; a will; a counseling plan; a proposal for settlement or agreement; a discovery plan; a witness examination plan; and a closing argument."[47]

Unlike other bar questions, the MPT tests a variety of skills acquired over the entire law school experience, with a special emphasis on legal writing. Skills acquired in contracts, trusts and estates, appellate advocacy, and alternative dispute resolution prove helpful in connection with the MPT. The analytical tools learned from briefing cases in class are also necessary.

In a separate setting, candidates for the bar also are required to take a test demonstrating proficiency in legal ethics.[48] This exam is known as the Multistate Professional Responsibility Examination ("MPRE"). The MPRE is a shorter exam, comparatively speaking, of a two-hour-and-five-minute duration.[49] It contains sixty multiple-choice questions. The principle law school course that prepares the candidate for the MPRE is professional responsibility, which is a required course in most law schools, offered in the second or third year of coursework.

A number of private companies offer bar review courses and study aids. Although the details of those courses are beyond the scope of this work, as indicated above, the authors highly recommend that a candidate for the bar take one or more such courses.

The Practice of Law

In addition to the core classes required of the bar, the authors recommend that law students strategically select courses to maximize employment in the student's desired field. The choices are somewhat obvious in some cases. For example, corporate lawyers to-be should take courses in business related classes such as a variety of tax courses including federal income tax, real estate law, and contract drafting courses. Future criminal lawyers should have a strong background in constitutional law, criminal law, criminal procedure, and appellate advocacy. Students who wish to have a trial practice should take courses in trial advocacy, appellate advocacy, alternative dispute resolution, pre-trial practice and procedure, and advanced topics in evidence. Those who desire to specialize in employment law should take courses in employment law, and labor law and federal courts among other classes. Students are encouraged to seek guidance from faculty and practicing lawyers in crafting a personal curriculum consistent with the career path anticipated.

Extracurricular Activities

In addition to coursework, law schools offer a variety of extracurricular opportunities that develop skills and create networking opportunities. Most employers evaluate employment candidates based on grades and extracurricular activities, although grades are emphasized.

There are a number of opportunities to consider. Law schools publish scholarly publications known as law reviews. Scholars and practitioners submit articles for consideration for publication and the members of the law review select articles and edit them for publication. Law review members also are given opportunities to publish student comments on the law. Serving as a member or editor on a law review, and getting published, are some of the most coveted extracurricular opportunities that law school offers. Work in putting together a high quality publication develops skills in legal writing and legal citations, which are the backbone of the practice of law.[50]

Law schools have student government opportunities as well. Students run for office in the Student Bar Associations ("SBA"). The SBA interacts with faculty and administration on student life and social functions of the student body. Many schools have disciplinary boards comprised of students and faculty. These are generally known as honor courts. Members of the honor court sit in judgment over students accused of academic dishonesty, among other infractions of school rules. Student government service is an honor that demonstrates leadership and trust to employers.

Law schools offer students the opportunity to compete in trials, competitions, appellate arguments, negotiation, mediation, client counseling, and most recently, arbitration advocacy. Students who excel in competitions are given the opportunity to compete on school-sponsored regional and national teams. Winning or placing prominently in school and national competitions is an excellent way to attract the attention of prospective employers.

Law schools offer a variety of other extracurricular opportunities that vary with each school's student body and emphasis. Students seeking to maximize employment opportunities should strive to get involved in extracurricular offerings. One caveat to consider: grades are still the primary hiring criteria for lawyers. Becoming too involved in extracurricular activities, at the expense of one's grades, should be avoided.

Clerkships

In the summer months following the first and second years of law school, and during the school year after the first year of law school,[51] students compete to earn clerkships at prestigious law firms. The aim of the student is twofold: earn money and potentially earn a full-time position post graduation.

Summer clerkships for top students can be particularly remunerative. Firms in large defense firms will pay in the neighborhood of $1,600 per week for summer work. Jobs are offered in full- or half-summer intervals. The summer clerkship is reminiscent of summer camp. Although students are expected to perform rudimentary legal work, the firm usually places the student in a number of social settings to get a feel for his or her personality and character. Alcohol is abundant, and self-control is warranted for obvious reasons. Depending on the locale, social events include a summer softball league, frequent cocktail and dinner parties with partners, white water rafting, and summer concert series. The quality of the student's work, coupled with their maturity and professional demeanor are criteria for evaluating the student's prospects for a job offer.

Most clerkships are substantially less glamorous, particularly clerkships offered during the school year, when the summer recruiting season is over. Students are paid ten to twenty dollars per hour for basic legal work (research projects, initial drafts of pleadings and discovery, etc.). Students can gain valuable work experience when clerking with firms. As most firms hire out of their clerkship programs, students are encouraged to obtain a clerkship at a desirable firm.

Golden Handcuffs: Managing Debt and Income Post Graduation

Many graduating law students will get themselves into trouble by overspending and under-saving. This problem naturally occurs for a variety of reasons. First, the typical graduate is around twenty-five or twenty-six years of age. In many cases, the new graduate has never held a professional job in his or her career, and consequently has meager experience in managing money. Second, living on student loans and borrowed money for seven or eight years, in many cases, will create an abundant desire to spend money once a job is acquired. Law students delay purchasing high-ticket items, such as cars and homes during school. However, the new lawyer has a perception that he or she will probably need better transportation, housing, and professional attire, in keeping with their newly acquired station in life. Third, our modern American culture promotes debt. Debt is peddled as a good thing because debt is the key to satisfying pent-up spending urges and impulsive consumer spending habits. Accumulating too much debt narrows employment options. Many young lawyers cannot change jobs because the mantle of debt has tied them inextricably to their job in "golden handcuffs."

Giving in to the urge to borrow more money is a serious personal mistake that could haunt the new lawyer for years. The best way to illustrate this point is through a fact specific illustration.

A starting salary of a typical new lawyer in America is around $65,000. To many young lawyers, a salary of $65,000 is very appealing and gratifying. However, a $65,000 salary is modest by cost of living standards. Student debt is a primary problem. Depending on whether the student attended public or private undergraduate and law school, average student debts range from around fifty to one hundred thousand dollars . A student with an educational debt of sixty thousand dollars can expect to pay around six hundred dollars per month for at least twenty years. A salary of around $65,000 will give the new lawyer a take home pay of around $3,400 per month, after taxes, 401k contributions and standard paycheck deductions such as insurance and parking. Subtracting the student loan payment of six hundred dollars from the take home pay of $3,400 leaves a balance of $2,800 to pay all other expenses, such as food, clothing, housing, car payments, and credit card debt that many students accumulate in college and law school, among other expenses. Purchasing a new home and car after graduation is not recommended for obvious reasons. Although many lawyers will become wealthy in the practice, most lawyers average only slightly more than one hundred thousand dollars per year in compensation during the course of their practice.

Young law students should avoid purchasing new cars and homes, and instead spend their money on reducing student debt, driving an affordable used car, and renting a home until a suitable down payment can be accumulated.

The Skills You Have Versus the Skills You Need

Good students sometimes make poor lawyers. The life of a successful student is vastly different from that of a successful lawyer. Many students plan their course selection around optimal work conditions—few early morning classes and no Friday classes. Students spend around sixteen hours per week attending class. Students are expected to spend about twice that time preparing for class. Grades are usually determined by one end-of-semester final exam. Students spend the days and weeks leading up to the exam by preparing outlines and cramming for tests. Success is largely measured in grade point averages.

The life of a practicing lawyer could not be more different. The first adjustment a young lawyer has to make is work schedule. Successful lawyers work fifty hours per week or more. The day begins with a morning commute around 6:30 or 7:00 a.m. The workday ends around 6:00 p.m. at the office, unless of course the lawyer has a major piece of work due, such as an important brief or a large transaction, in which case the workday can extend for hours. Most lawyers work at least sometimes on weekends.

Law students live in a world of grades and professors. Lawyers must navigate a world of cash flow and clients. Law is a business. Unfortunately, law school offers almost no courses on the business of law. Shamefully, most graduating lawyers cannot interpret a balance sheet or profit and loss statement. Almost none know the difference between accounts receivables and work in progress. Legal training completely neglects the economics of the practice of law, which is the key to a successful practice. So, what is a prospective lawyer to do? The obvious answer is to take more business and accounting classes as part of a balanced undergraduate experience. For those of us who majored in history or political science, do not despair; there are other ways to fill in the gaps.

Lawyers working in private practice will spend the first five to ten years working as an associate in a firm. Associates are employees who work under the partners or shareholders of firms. The associate experience is not unlike the training doctors receive in their first few years of residency. Associates learn how to practice law in these formative years. An astute associate will strive to develop the necessary skills for future partnership in the firm. There are three basic things that every lawyer in private practice must do: Get work (attracting and keep clients); do work successfully; and be profitable. Unfortunately, most firms center associate training on "doing work" as opposed to getting work and managing cash flow. It is worth mentioning that very few lawyers actually perform all three skills well. This is one reason why lawyers tend to band together in firms. Successful firms will have rainmakers (those who can attract top clients), workers (those who complete the work), and managers (those who work "on" the business as opposed to "in" it). The need to run a practice like a business has caused a new professional segment to emerge—professional law firm managers, who understand accounting and the economics of the practice of law.

Law firms usually do a poor job of training lawyers to be good business managers. This is the case because the owners of a firm generally like to keep the books confidential from the employees. A young associate does not get much of an opportunity to review the firm's financial data and ask a lot of questions. Nevertheless, young lawyers should take every opportunity to learn the business when such an inquiry will not be viewed as impolitic by firm management.

Young lawyers seeking partnership, however, must have some basic aptitude in all three skills. Which skill is the most important? If maximum compensation is the aim of the lawyer, then attracting and keeping clients is the most important skill. A lawyer with fifteen years of experience seeking to change firms will generally be asked one important question, above all others: How much business do you have? If the answer is, "little or none, but I do great work," then the chances of getting another job are not good. Grade point averages from law school are not emphasized or even discussed in these settings. Of course, this observation is not intended to disparage the skills of great practitioners or business minds. Indeed, rainmakers are often thought of as larger than life attorneys, who must surround themselves with excellent legal technicians and business managers to succeed. The point is that young lawyers should aim to create proficiencies in all three arenas.

A discussion of successful skills necessary to practice law would be incomplete without a brief discussion of technology. Computers emerged in the legal business in the early 1990s. At first, only legal secretaries used DOS based word programming software to create documents. Few senior lawyers used computers or could even type proficiently.

The tech revolution that characterized the 90s changed everything. Companies like Westlaw and Lexis/Nexis rolled out electronic databases for legal resources, such as case law and statutes. The advent of these technologies quickly rendered large law firm libraries almost obsolete.

Other software began to permeate the practice. Sophisticated accounting software for law firms emerged as well, which created greater efficiencies in accounting. Thereafter, software companies created case management software. Modern case management software is extremely powerful. One program can capture and organize large legal files, including client documents, legal research, pleadings, correspondence, depositions, and so on. Furthermore, the Internet now enables practitioners to practice law remotely from a laptop computer anywhere in the world. One of the authors recently taught a course in Cambridge, England and successfully practiced law on a laptop computer for over a month. E-mail, coupled with remote access to all electronic files makes such an endeavor practical (although, admittedly, wireless access is still expensive).

Most lawyers now use multi-function phones, like BlackBerry, to keep up with e-mails, answer client calls, and access electronic calendars. Devices like these are standard in the business world, and clients now demand that lawyers use these tools to provide greater service.

The court systems are beginning to use technology to create efficiencies. All federal courts and most state courts in the country now have electronic filing software. Instead of mailing pleadings to a clerk's office for filing the old fashioned way, lawyers now can file pleadings electronically, by using software hosted by the court system.

The latest trend in legal software is electronic trial software. Several companies now promote software that is designed to organize and display evidence in court. The days of shuffling five-by-seven photos to a jury are over. Software now permits lawyers to play videos in court and to display documents and photos on large projector screens for the benefit of the judge and jury.

Every prospective lawyer should strive to become "tech-savvy." Proficiency in Word, Excel, and e-mail programs is not sufficient. Every young lawyer needs a basic familiarity with legal research tools, like Westlaw, in addition to accounting software (to record time entries), case management software, and ultimately electronic trial software.

Job Satisfaction and Attrition: The Expectations Problem

Joseph Story, a former Harvard Law professor, once remarked, "The law is a jealous mistress and requires a long and constant courtship."[52] Those of us with practice experience fully appreciate this observation because a successful career in law demands long hours of hard work. Somehow, American pop culture has overlooked this important point. The portrayal of lawyers on television, and in cinema, has created a "disconnect" between fantasy and reality in the minds of law students and young lawyers, which ultimately can lead to job dissatisfaction. Each generation has its iconic legal protagonists (Perry Mason, Matlock, lawyers from LA Law, and most recently Boston Legal). Their lives appear important, their incomes extravagant, and their successes in trial abundant and newsworthy. Sharing cocktails with Denny Crain on the balcony of an up-scale Boston high-rise seems glamorous and attainable to the minds of many lawyers to-be.

The problem, however, is that pop culture portrayals of lawyers are pure fantasy. Very few first-year lawyers will ever see the inside of a courtroom. Even experienced litigators are finding jury trials less common; few lawyers try more than five or six cases per year. A typical day in the life of a young litigator usually entails a ten-hour day of answering e-mails from superiors, performing research projects, and answering discovery (i.e., the least glamorous and most unpleasant work to be had in a firm). Client contact is rare, as most young lawyers spend their days staring at a computer monitor. The shift from law school life to a fifty-plus-hour week lifestyle is daunting. Add to that the additional layer of having to account for six-minute increments of every hour of every day for billing purposes (the notorious "billable hour"), and it's no wonder that even the most idealistic young lawyer finds the practice of law to be tedious and unfulfilling. The obvious problem is an issue of perception: What law students "think" lawyers do versus the reality of practice. The startling realization that the practice of law is vastly different from naïve expectations leads many young lawyers to change jobs in search of a more fulfilling life, or abandon the practice altogether.

A recent study published by the American Bar Association reports the following not-so-surprising trends. The news is not all bad, but the disturbing statistic that young lawyers usually do not remain long with their first employers is a telling trend that bears out the fact that young lawyers, similar to other professionals, find the practice of their professions disappointing in some respects.

- A median billable year is 1,860 hours.[53]
- One-half of young lawyers spend more than fifty hours per week on legal work.
- Most young lawyers are at least somewhat satisfied both with their current job and with the practice of law generally.
- More than seven out of ten are at least somewhat satisfied with the balance between their professional and personal lives.
- Among those in private practice, small-firm practitioners are more likely than those in larger firms to find that their expectations are being met with regard to their ability to contribute to the social good, help others, and enjoy a certain quality of life. On the other hand, larger-firm practitioners are more likely to experience greater financial rewards and significant potential for advancement.

- Despite a high level of overall satisfaction with current position and the practice of law generally, more than sixty-five percent indicated that they would consider switching jobs within two years.[54]

Indeed, a recent survey reports that almost 80 percent of young lawyers at large law firms no longer work there after five years.[55] Many undergraduate students attend law school because they are good students generally, have not weighed other career options seriously, and have only a vague understanding of what lawyers really do.[56] If this sentiment sounds familiar, then the authors encourage the reader to evaluate career options more carefully. A prospective law student should weigh the reality of the practice of law fully before undertaking the expense and time commitment of legal training.

Partnership: The Holy Grail?

In private practice, young lawyers strive to become partners. Partnership has become the quintessential Holy Grail. In large defense firms, for example, partnership is generally offered after a period of years. In small-to-medium-sized cities, partnership track is five to seven years. In larger cities partnership track extends into the eight- to ten-year time period. There are different kinds of partners in law firms. Non-equity partners are those who generally do not own a financial stake in the firm but who have, nevertheless, completed a satisfactory associateship at the firm. Equity partnership is preferred as it denotes ownership and some control in firm decisions.

This model of partnership acquisition is somewhat deceptive as it camouflages the appropriate goals of a young associate. Every young associate needs to focus on the twin aims of developing competency and clients. Competency is generally achieved in five to eight years. However, client development is not a function of years in service; rather, it is dependent totally on the drive and hard work of the young associate. Client development is a relationship business. Young associates should spend their time getting to know judges, other lawyers (who are excellent sources of business), and business people. A person's ability to generate work, while certainly dependent on competency, is much more dependent on making and managing long term quality relationships.

In the view of the authors, many young associates never achieve partnership because they overlook the fact that partners must assume a financial role in the firm, and that doing so requires having independent sources of legal work tied to the aspiring partner.

The marketing concept of "branding" has now made its way into legal circles. A lawyer's "brand" is the sum total of their reputation among the bench, bar, and the community at large. Young associates who wish to become partners should strive to maximize their "brand" by always conducting themselves professionally among judges and other lawyers, and by performing superior legal work at a fair price. The majority of lawyers obtain and keep long-term clients not through tacky television commercials, but rather through long years of dedicated and quality service to the community. Over time, as a young lawyer's skill set grows, he or she will inevitably develop a niche practice where the lawyer obtains a high degree of skill in a particular field of law or type of case. Small town lawyers tend to be generalist, while lawyers in larger cities tend to specialize their skills to offer high quality services to a narrow range of clients.

So, although partnership may be the "Holy Grail" to young associates, it should not be the ultimate aim of practice life. The young associate should focus on competency and quality relationships as a more desirable aim. Such an approach will ultimately lead to partnership.

The Evolution of a Practice

Most young lawyers are not prepared to practice law when they enter the work force. Starting lawyers have few if any clients, rudimentary courtroom skills, and no sense of tactics or strategy. Most young lawyers are poor brief writers and must strive mightily to avoid the ever-present threat of malpractice. For these reasons, it should come as no surprise that young lawyers need to work for other lawyers to develop the skills necessary to not only achieve competence in the law, but emerge with sound legal and business judgment. The skills necessary to succeed in private practice are many and some skills develop more quickly than others.

The first five to seven years of law practice need to be spent gaining competence and experience. Shadowing an able practitioner is the best way to learn these skills. Young lawyers, in the first couple of years of practice, are generally not permitted to serve important pleadings or mail important correspondence without approval from the lawyer managing the file. Law has its own distinct language; most young lawyers learn this. What they lack, however, is an understanding of tactics and strategy necessary to develop a case from start to finish.

Most firms train lawyers by providing them with pieces of cases in project format. A young lawyer may be asked to answer discovery, draft pleadings, and the like. The goal is to give the young lawyer work that they are suited to complete. After years of handling bits and pieces of cases, an experienced lawyer is generally able to manage a case from start to finish. There is no rule of thumb, as case complexity inevitably drives decision making. In reality, most new lawyers will not be trusted with complete case management for at least three to five years.

Some skills develop more slowly than others. Effective interrogation in deposition is a skill that takes years to cultivate. For this reason, many large firms place minimum experience guidelines on the taking of depositions. For example, one large firm in Birmingham has the following experience rule: Associates with five years experience or less may take or defend nonparty depositions. Senior associates (experience in the five- to seven-year range) may take or defend party depositions. Partners may take expert witness depositions.

Again, there is no hard and fast rule, but sensible guidelines become self-evident to seasoned lawyers who have seen young people fail when given inappropriate responsibility.

Associates who intend to be seriously considered for partnership need to begin cultivating clients as soon as possible. Because ethical constraints limit in-person and print advertisements in the legal field, developing business can take years to achieve. Young lawyers should be encouraged to join the local and state bar organizations to develop networking opportunities with other lawyers, who are excellent sources of business through referral networks. As associates garner experience, many firms will assign responsibility over smaller clients to such associates. The goal is to acquire a book of business sufficient to support the associate and his or her overhead. Associates who do so are looked upon favorably for partnership. Those who fail in this endeavor are sometimes asked to resign or are offered non-equity positions in the firm.

One of the last skills to develop is business management experience. As associates pass into the ranks of partnership they are given more responsibility for leadership; such as being offered roles on firm committees. Over time, associates learn the ins and outs of financial accounting matters. Once these skills are mastered, the lawyer is in the position to assume full management responsibilities in a firm. The scope of that discussion is beyond this work. However, prospective lawyers need to be mindful of the types of skills necessary for firm leadership and success.

Epilogue

The foregoing materials offered practical information concerning preparing for a legal education and the difficulty that one will encounter in pursuing such. Advice was also offered relating to how one can achieve success as a law student, with discussion of study materials, as well as preparation for class and examinations. The concluding portion of the text offered a realistic approach to both the pitfalls and strategies for obtaining success one should recognize in becoming a viable member of the legal profession.

Throughout the book, the authors sought to present the opportunity to become a lawyer as both difficult and that which should not be undertaken by less than a capable and dedicated student. The reader should not conclude that the authors are advising one not to seek a legal education. On the contrary, the authors are attempting to provide prospective lawyers with practical information that will aid them in achieving their dreams. Further, one should recognize that legal education is unique in that many competent and dedicated students complete the rigorous legal education curriculum and ultimately use their legal education in ways other than law practice.

A legal education is an intellectual endeavour that offers the student an opportunity to mature as a member of the American culture intellectually and practically. Members of the bar in every state of America are leaders in government and business, as well as legal practitioners. The very future of the American culture depends upon the existence of highly motivated citizens, including competent lawyers serving in the practice of law and other segments of our culture necessary to America's participatory government. There is not, in the opinion of the authors, a more necessary and honourable profession in which one can become involved.

Appendix A:

Comparative Tuition Expense for Selected Private and State Supported Law Schools[57]

School Academic Year Tuition
Yale Law School
Data Source: www.law.yale.edu/admissions/costs.htm
$44,000

Baylor Law School
Data Source: www.baylor.edu/sfs/index.php?id=70196
$13,048 per quarter
$13,048 x 3= $39,144

Georgia State Law School
Data Source: http://law.gsu.edu/admissions/tuition.php
Resident: $10,296
Non-Resident: $31,320

University of Alabama
http://www.top-law-schools.com/alabama-school-of-law.html
Resident: $14,450
Non-Resident: $26,560

Cumberland School of Law, Samford University
http://cumberland.samford.edu/admissions/financial-aid-scholarships
$32,900

Note: Interested readers should view each web page for approximated total budgets, including books, fees and living expenses.

Appendix B

Roster of American Bar Association Approved Law Schools As of June 2008 (* Provisionally approved)

University of Akron
C. Blake McDowell Law Center
http://www.uakron.edu/law/

University of Alabama School of Law
http://www.law.ua.edu/

Albany Law School
http://www.albanylaw.edu/

American University
Washington College of Law
http://www.wcl.american.edu/

Appalachian School of Law
http://www.asl.edu/

University of Arizona
James E. Rogers College of Law
http://www.law.arizona.edu/

Arizona State University
Sandra Day O'Connor College of Law
http://www.law.asu.edu/

University of Arkansas School of Law
http://law.uark.edu/

University of Arkansas at Little Rock
William H. Bowen School of Law
http://www.law.ualr.edu/

Atlanta's John Marshall Law School
http://www.johnmarshall.edu/

Ave Maria School of Law
http://www.avemarialaw.edu/

University of Baltimore School of Law
http://law.ubalt.edu/

Barry University
Dwayne O. Andreas School of Law
http://www.barry.edu/law/

Baylor Law School
http://law.baylor.edu/

Boston College Law School
http://www.bc.edu/schools/law/home.html

Boston University School of Law
http://www.bu.edu/law/

Brigham Young University
J. Reuben Clark Law School
http://www.law .byu.edu/

Brooklyn Law School
http://www.brooklaw.edu/

University of California Berkeley School of Law
http://www.law.berkeley.edu/

University of California Davis School of Law
http://www.law.ucdavis.edu/

University of California Hastings College of the Law
http://www.uchastings.edu/

University of California Los Angeles School of Law
http://www.law.ucla.edu/home/Default.aspx

California Western School of Law
http://www.cwsl.edu/main/home.asp

Campbell University
Norman Adrian Wiggins School of Law
http://www.law.campbell.edu/

Capital University Law School
http://www.law.capital.edu/

Case Western Reserve University
Franklin T. Backus School of Law
http://law.case.edu/

Catholic University of America
Columbus School of Law
http://www.law.edu/

Chapman University School of Law
http://www.chapman.edu/law/

Charleston School of Law*
http://www.charlestonlaw.org/

Charlotte School of Law*
http://www.charlottelaw.org/

University of Chicago Law School
http://www.law.uchicago.edu/

Chicago-Kent College of Law
Illinois Institute of Technology
http://www.kentlaw.edu/

University of Cincinnati College of Law
http://www.law.uc.edu/

City University of New York
School of Law at Queens College
http://www.law.cuny.edu/index.html

Cleveland State University
Cleveland Marshall College of Law
http://www.law.csuohio.edu/

University of Colorado School of Law
http://www.colorado.edu/law/

Columbia University School of Law
http://www.law.columbia.edu/

University of Connecticut School of Law
http://www.law.uconn.edu/

Cornell Law School
http://www.lawschool.cornell.edu/

Creighton University School of Law
http://www.creighton.edu/law/

University of Dayton School of Law
http://law.udayton.edu/

University of Denver
Sturm College of Law
http://www.law.du.edu/

DePaul University College of Law
http://www.law.depaul.edu/

University of Detroit Mercy School of Law
http://www.law.udmercy.edu/

University of District of Columbia
David A. Clarke School of Law
http://www.law.udc.edu/

Drake University Law School
http://www.law.drake.edu/

Drexel University*
Earle Mack School of Law
http://www.drexel.edu/law/

Duke University School of Law
http://www.law.duke.edu/

Dusquesne University School of Law
http://www.law.duq.edu/

Elon University School of Law*
http://www.elon.edu/e-web/law/

Emory University School of Law
http://www.law.emory.edu/

Faulkner University
Thomas Goode Jones School of Law
http://www.faulkner.edu/admissions/jonesLaw.asp

University of Florida
Fredric G. Levin College of Law
http://www.law.ufl.edu/

Florida A & M University College of Law
http://www.famu.edu/index.cfm?a=law

Florida Coastal School of Law
http://www.fcsl.edu/

Florida International University College of Law
http://law.fiu.edu/

Florida State University College of Law
http://www.law.fsu.edu/

Fordham University School of Law
http://law.fordham.edu/index.htm

Franklin Pierce Law Center
http://www.piercelaw.edu/

George Mason University School of Law
http://www.law.gmu.edu/

The George Washington University Law School
http://www.law.gwu.edu/Pages/Default.aspx

Georgetown University Law Center
http://www.law.georgetown.edu/

University of Georgia School of Law
http://www.lawsch.uga.edu/

Georgia State University College of Law
http://law.gsu.edu/

Golden Gate University School of Law
http://www.ggu.edu/school_of_law

Gonzaga University School of Law
http://www.law.gonzaga.edu/

Hamline University School of Law
http://law.hamline.edu/

Harvard University Law School
http://www.law.harvard.edu/index.html

University of Hawaii
William S. Richardson School of Law
http://www.hawaii.edu/law/

Hofstra University School of Law
http://law.hofstra.edu/home/index.html

University of Houston Law Center
http://www.law.uh.edu/homepage.html

Howard University School of Law
http://www.law.howard.edu/

University of Idaho College of Law
http://www.law.uidaho.edu/default.aspx?pid=

University of Illinois College of Law
http://www.law.uiuc.edu/

Indiana University School of Law, Bloomington
http://www.law.indiana.edu/

Indiana University School of Law, Indianapolis
http://indylaw.indiana.edu/

Inter American University of Puerto Rico
http://www.derecho.inter.edu/

University of Iowa College of Law
http://www.law.uiowa.edu/

The John Marshall Law School
http://www.jmls.edu/

Judge Advocate General's Legal Center & School
US Army
http://www.jagcnet.army.mil/tjagsa

The University of Kansas School of Law
http://www.law.ku.edu/

University of Kentucky College of Law
http://www.uky.edu/Law/

University of LaVerne College of Law*
http://law.ulv.edu/

Lewis & Clark Law School
http://law.lclark.edu/

Liberty University School of Law*
http://law.liberty.edu/

Louisiana State University
Paul M. Hebert Law Center
http://www.law.lsu.edu/

University of Louisville
Louis D. Brandeis School of Law
http://www.law.louisville.edu/

Loyola Law School
http://www.lls.edu/

Loyola University- Chicago School of Law
http://www.luc.edu/law/

Loyola University -New Orleans College of Law
http://law.loyno.edu/

University of Maine School of Law
http://mainelaw.maine.edu/

Marquette University Law School
http://law.marquette.edu/cgi-bin/site.pl

The University of Maryland School of Law
http://www.law.umaryland.edu/index.html

University of the Pacific
McGeorge School of Law
http://www.mcgeorge.edu/

The University of Memphis
Cecil C. Humphreys School of Law
http://www.law.memphis.edu/

Mercer University
Walter F. George School of Law
http://www.law.mercer.edu/

University of Miami School of Law
http://www.law.miami.edu/

The University of Michigan Law School
http://www.law.umich.edu/Pages/default.aspx

Michigan State University College of Law
http://www.law.msu.edu/

The University of Minnesota Law School
http://www.law.umn.edu/

University of Mississippi School of Law
http://www.law.olemiss.edu/

Mississippi College School of Law
http://law.mc.edu/

University of Missouri-Columbia School of Law
http://www.law.missouri.edu/

University of Missouri- Kansas City School of Law
http://www.law.umkc.edu/

The University of Montana School of Law
http://www.umt.edu/law/

The University of Nebraska
Lincoln College of Law
http://law.unl.edu/home

University of Nevada Las Vegas
William S. Boyd School of Law
http://www.law.unlv.edu/

New England School of Law
http://www.nesl.edu/

University of New Mexico School of Law
http://lawschool.unm.edu/

New York Law School
http://www.nyls.edu/

New York University School of Law
http://www.law.nyu.edu/index.htm

University of North Carolina School of Law
http://www.law.unc.edu/

North Carolina Central University School of Law
http://www.acc.nccu.edu/law/

The University of North Dakota School of Law
http://www.law.und.nodak.edu/

Northeastern University School of Law
http://www.slaw.neu.edu/

Northern Illinois University College of Law
http://law.niu.edu/law/

Northern Kentucky University
Salmon P. Chase College of Law
http://www.nku.edu/~chase/

Northwestern University School of Law
http://www.law.northwestern.edu/

University of Notre Dame Law School
http://law.nd.edu/

Nova Southeastern University
Shepard Broad Law Center
http://www.nsulaw.nova.edu/

Ohio Northern University
Claude W. Pettit College of Law
http://www.law.onu.edu/

Ohio State University
Michael E. Moritz College of Law
http://moritzlaw.osu.edu/

The University of Oklahoma College of Law
http://www.law.ou.edu/

Oklahoma City University School of Law
http://www.okcu.edu/law/

University of Oregon School of Law
http://www.law.uoregon.edu/

Pace University School of Law
http://www.law.pace.edu/

University of Pennsylvania Law School
http://www.law.upenn.edu/

Pennsylvania State
Dickinson School of Law
http://www.dsl.psu.edu/

Pepperdine University
Odell McConnell Law Center
http://law.pepperdine.edu/

Phoenix School of Law*
http://www.phoenixlaw.edu/

University of Pittsburgh School of Law
http://www.law.pitt.edu/

Pontifical Catholic University of Puerto Rico
Faculty of Law
http://www.pucpr.edu/

University of Puerto Rico School of Law
http://upracd.upr.clu.edu/derecho.htm

Quinnipiac University School of Law
http://law.quinnipiac.edu/

Regent University School of Law
http://www.regent.edu/acad/schlaw/

University of Richmond
T.C. Williams School of Law
http://law.richmond.edu/

Roger Williams University School of Law
http://law.rwu.edu/

Rutgers University School of Law-Camden
http://www-camlaw.rutgers.edu/

Rutgers School of Law-Newark
http://law.newark.rutgers.edu//

Saint Louis University School of Law
http://lawlib.slu.edu/

Samford University
Cumberland School of Law
http://cumberland.samford.edu/

University of San Diego School of Law
http://www.sandiego.edu/usdlaw/

University of San Francisco School of Law
http://www.usfca.edu/law/

Santa Clara University School of Law
http://law.scu.edu/

Seattle University School of Law
http://www.law.seattleu.edu/

Seton Hall University School of Law
http://law.shu.edu/

University of South Carolina School of Law
http://www.law.sc.edu/

The University of South Dakota School of Law
http://www.usd.edu/law/

South Texas College of Law
http://www.stcl.edu/

University of Southern California
Gould School of Law
http://lawweb.usc.edu/

Southern Illinois University School of Law
http://www.law.siu.edu/

Southern Methodist University
Dedman School of law
http://www.law.smu.edu/

Southern University Law Center
http://www.sulc.edu/index_ie.htm

Southwestern Law School
http://www.swlaw.edu/

St. John's University School of Law
http://new.stjohns.edu/academics/graduate/law

St. Mary's University School of Law
http://www.stmarytx.edu/law/

University of St. Thomas School of Law
http://www.stthomas.edu/law/

St. Thomas University School of Law
http://www.stu.edu/Default.aspx?alias=www.stu.edu/law

Stanford Law School
http://www.law.stanford.edu/

State University of New York at Buffalo Law School
http://www.law.buffalo.edu/

Stetson University College of Law
http://www.law.stetson.edu/

Suffolk University Law School
http://www.law.suffolk.edu/

Syracuse University College of Law
http://www.law.syr.edu/

Temple University
James E. Beasley School of Law
http://www.law.temple.edu/

The University of Tennessee College of Law
http://www.law.utk.edu/

The University of Texas School of Law
http://www.utexas.edu/law/

Texas Southern University
Thurgood Marshall School of Law
http://www.tsulaw.edu/

Texas Tech University School of Law
http://www.law.ttu.edu/

Texas Wesleyan University School of Law
http://www.law.txwes.edu/

Thomas Jefferson School of Law
http://www.tjsl.edu/

Thomas M. Cooley Law School
http://www.cooley.edu/

The University of Toledo College of Law
http://law.utoledo.edu/

Touro College
Jacob D. Fuchsberg Law Center
http://www.tourolaw.edu/

Tulane University School of Law
http://www.law.tulane.edu/

The University of Tulsa College of Law
http://www.law.utulsa.edu/

The University of Utah
S.J. Quinney College of Law
http://www.law.utah.edu/

Valparaiso University School of Law
http://www.valpo.edu/law/

Vanderbilt University School of Law
http://law.vanderbilt.edu/index.aspx

Vermont Law School
http://www.vermontlaw.edu/

Villanova University School of Law
http://www.law.villanova.edu/

University of Virginia School of Law
http://www.law.virginia.edu/html/index.htm

Wake Forest University School of Law
http://law.wfu.edu/

Washburn University School of Law
http://washburnlaw.edu/

University of Washington School of Law
http://www.law.washington.edu/

Washington & Lee University School of Law
http://www.law.wlu.edu/

Washington University School of Law
http://www.wulaw.wustl.edu/

Wayne State University Law School
http://www.law.wayne.edu/

West Virginia University College of Law
http://law.wvu.edu/

Western New England College School of Law
http://www . aw.wnec.edu/

Western State University College of Law*
http://www.wsulaw.edu/index.asp

Whittier Law School
http://www.law.whittier.edu/

Widener University School of Law
http://law.widener.edu/

Willamette University College of Law
http://www.willamette.edu/wucl/

College of William and Mary
Marshall -Wythe Law School
http://web.wm.edu/law/?&=&svr=www

William Mitchell College of Law
http://www.wmitchell.edu/

University of Wisconsin Law School
http://www.law.wisc.edu/

University of Wyoming College of Law
http://uwadmnweb.uwyo.edu/Law/

Yale Law School
http://www.law.yale.edu/

Yeshiva University
Benjamin N. Cardozo School of Law
http://www.cardozo.yu.edu/

Appendix C

Example Law Examination, Including Both Analytical and Multistate Questions

Final Examination
Fall 2008
Alternative Dispute Resolution
Law 647–01
Professor W. Scott Simpson
Student Number:__________________________________

This is your final examination. It consists of 25 multiple choice questions, five (5) short answer questions and one 2-part essay question. The multiple choice questions should be answered on a scantron sheet. The essay and short answer questions may be answered either in the space provided below or in a separate document (for those of you who choose to type your exam answers). With regard to the short answer and essay questions, your answers will be graded based on legal analysis, conciseness and thoroughness. You have three (3) hours to complete the examination. You may not use your books and notes when taking the test.

Multiple Choice Questions (These are worth 2 points each).

1. Which of the following are types of alternative dispute resolution techniques?
   (a) Mediations.
   (b) Second party evaluations.
   (c) Jury trials.
   (d) All of the above.

2. When a mediator helps parties and their counsel assess likely outcomes by inquiring into the legal and factual strengths and weakness of the problems presented, the mediator is engaging in:
   (a) Evaluative mediation.
   (b) Facilitative mediation.
   (c) Outcome mediation.
   (d) Assessment mediation.

3. Which of the following is not a part of a typical mediation process?
   (a) Mediator's introduction.
   (b) Issue identification.
   (c) Option generation.
   (d) A final award.

4. A motion to compel arbitration is in the nature of:
   (a) A motion for summary judgment on an action for specific performance.
   (b) A motion to dismiss based on an action for rescission.
   (c) A legal action for contract enforcement.
   (d) An equitable action for rescission.

5. The legal doctrine which provides that agreements to arbitrate may be canceled by either side until the arbitration award is rendered is known as the:
   (a) Doctrine of mutuality of remedy.
   (b) Doctrine of functus officio.
   (c) Doctrine of revocability.
   (d) Doctrine of separability.

6. Modern arbitration law has its origins in the:
   (a) Kansas Arbitration Act.
   (b) New York Arbitration Act.
   (c) California Arbitration Act.
   (d) Illinois Arbitration Act.

7. The Federal Arbitration Act:
   (a) Is considered a federal question for purposes of federal jurisdiction.
   (b) Is not considered a federal question for purposes of federal jurisdiction.
   (c) Always serves as a basis for federal jurisdiction whenever the amount in controversy exceeds $75,000.
   (d) Is a basis for federal jurisdiction when an award is sought to be enforced.

8. Under the Bazzle decision:
   (a) A plaintiff/claimant can always demand class-wide arbitration.
   (b) The question of whether class arbitration is permitted is a function of state contract law.
   (c) Silent arbitration agreements are not subject to class action treatment in arbitration.
   (d) State and federal class action rules were determined to have no application in arbitrations.

9. Under modern jurisprudence, the Federal Arbitration Act:
   (a) May not be applied by state courts.
   (b) May be applied by state courts if state law provides for arbitration.
   (c) Must be applied by state courts if interstate commerce is involved and affected.
   (d) Must be applied by state courts if intrastate commerce is involved and affected.

10. Which of the following is a false statement:
    (a) The Federal Arbitration Act preempts state law restrictions on arbitration when the controversy involves or affects interstate commerce.
    (b) Under Alabama law, a pre-dispute binding arbitration agreement may be enforced pursuant to state statute.
    (c) Federal decisions interpreting the Federal Arbitration Act are considered federal common law.
    (d) The Federal Arbitration Act applies in consumer-related disputes that involve or affect interstate commerce.

11. Which of the following statement(s) is true:
    (a) Arbitration is a matter of a contract, and a party can only be required to submit to arbitration when the party has agreed to it in writing.
    (b) There is a liberal federal policy favoring arbitration agreements.
    (c) The Federal Arbitration Act establishes substantive federal law that must be consulted in determining whether or to what extent a given contract provides for arbitration.
    (d) All of the above.

12. Which of the following is not an accurate statement of law:
    (a) The Alabama Supreme Court decision, Sisters of the Visitation v Cochran Plastering Company, Inc. represents the modern view for determining interstate commerce under the Federal Arbitration Act.
    (b) Sisters of the Visitation v. Cochran Plastering Company, Inc. was rejected by the United States Supreme Court decision, Citizens Bank v. Alafabco, Inc.
    (c) The contemplation of the parties test, once embraced by Alabama jurisprudence is no longer an accepted doctrine for determining interstate commerce questions under the Federal Arbitration Act.
    (d) The Commerce Clause of the US Constitution gave Congress the power to enact the Federal Arbitration Act.

13. Arbitration agreements set forth in consumer warranties are:
    (a) Unenforceable because the Magnuson Moss Act preempts the Federal Arbitration Act.
    (b) Unenforceable because Arbitration Agreements are considered informal dispute resolution agreements under the Federal Trade Commission Regulations.
    (c) Enforceable because the Magnuson Moss Act was repealed by the Federal Arbitration Act.
    (d) Enforceable because the Magnuson Moss Act does not preclude binding arbitration under the Federal Arbitration Act.

14. Arbitration agreements are generally considered to be:
    (a) Choice of venue clauses.
    (b) Choice of forum clauses.
    (c) Informal dispute resolution mechanisms under applicable law.
    (d) Choice of law clauses.

15. In determining whether Congress intended to preclude arbitration of a statutory claim under Shearson/American Express, Inc. v. McMahon, the Supreme Court considers three (3) factors in deducing congressional intent. Which of the following is not one of those factors:
    (a) The text of the statute.
    (b) The legislative history of the statute.
    (c) Whether there is an inherent conflict between arbitration and the underlying purpose of the statute.
    (d) Administrative agency interpretations.

16. An arbitration award may be set aside by a court based on arbitrator bias if the party challenging the award proves:

    (a) The mere appearance of bias or partiality.

    (b) A reasonable impression or partiality, proven by direct and definite evidence.

    (c) Clear and convincing evidence of partiality based on subjective evidence.

    (d) Evident partiality proven beyond a reasonable doubt under the reasonable man standard.

17. An arbitration award may be set aside if the party challenging the award:

    (a) Establishes that her due process rights were violated.

    (b) Establishes that the arbitrator abused her discretion.

    (c) A & B.

    (d) None of the above.

18. Which of the following would not increase a party's chances of overturning an arbitration award:

    (a) A transcript of the arbitration proceeding.

    (b) A reasoned award.

    (c) A simple award.

    (d) A requirement that the arbitrator provide written findings of fact and conclusions of law.

19. Prior to the Federal Arbitration Act:
    (a) There was considerable judicial hostility against arbitration.
    (b) The common law favored arbitration of civil actions.
    (c) Federal courts favored arbitration, but state courts disallowed arbitration in almost all circumstances.
    (d) Arbitration was not the subject of jurisprudence because it was first invented in the 1930's.

20. In Alabama:
    (a) Pre-dispute binding arbitration agreements are enforceable pursuant to state statute.
    (b) Pre-dispute binding arbitration agreements are enforceable pursuant to state decisional law.
    (c) Post-dispute binding arbitration agreements are enforceable pursuant to state statute.
    (d) Post-dispute binding arbitration agreements are not enforceable pursuant to Title 8 of the Alabama Code.

21. A court will refuse to enforce an arbitration award governed by a collective bargaining agreement when:
    (a) Interstate commerce is involved and affected.
    (b) The award draws its essence from the collective bargaining agreement.
    (c) The award does not draw its essence from the collective bargaining agreement.
    (d) The arbitrator commits serious error, but arguably construes or applies the collective bargaining agreement within the scope of his authority.

22. In 2007, which of the following was not a valid ground for appealing an arbitration award in Alabama?
    (a) An argument that the arbitrator manifestly disregarded the law.
    (b) An argument that the arbitrator abused his discretion.
    (c) An argument that the arbitrator entered an award that was influenced by corruption, fraud or undue means.
    (d) An argument that the arbitrator exceeded his powers or imperfectly executed his powers such that a mutual, final and definite award upon the subject matter submitted was not made.

23. A range of processes in which an impartial person helps parties to a dispute to communicate and to make voluntary, informed choices in an effort to resolve their dispute is called:
    (a) Binding arbitration.
    (b) Non-binding arbitration.
    (c) A mini-trial.
    (d) Mediation.

24. Facts about a case that are divulged during a mediation:
    (a) Are independently discoverable and admissible in evidence as long as the mediation process itself is not the subject of discovery.
    (b) Are discoverable and admissible as long as both parties agree to allow the mediator to testify.
    (c) Are discoverable and admissible as long as the mediator consents to testify.
    (d) Are absolutely protected from discovery, and are not independently discoverable.

25. In Alabama:
    (a) If a party files a motion for mediation in court, the court should order mediation and the moving party must pay the costs of mediation.
    (b) If a party files a motion for mediation in court, the court may order mediation based on an analysis of three (3) factors set forth in Ala. Code Section 6–6-20, and the moving party must pay the costs of mediation if mediation is ordered.
    (c) If a party files a motion for mediation in court, the court must order mediation, and the parties must share the cost of mediation, unless they otherwise agree.
    (d) There is no legal basis to file a motion for mediation. Mediation, by its nature, must be consented to freely under the law.

Short Answer Questions. (These are worth 5 points each). Answer in the space provided under each question, or (if typing your answer), answer the question on a separate sheet of paper. If typing, please limit your answer to one-half (1/2) of a page per question.

1. Does the Supreme Court's decision in Hall Street Assoc. v. Mattell, Inc. limit grounds for appealing arbitration awards? Explain.

2. Explain the separability doctrine.

3. What is the best way to combat a person employing a hard positional bargaining approach in a negotiation?

4. In Alabama, are arbitration agreements, which are silent on the issue of class actions, subject to class action treatment? Explain by discussing relevant authority.

5. How does the timing of mediation affect the likelihood of successfully reaching a negotiated settlement through the mediation process?

Essay Question. This is a 2-part question. (Each part is worth 12.5 points, for a total of 25 points). Answer in the space provided, or (if typing your answer), answer the question on a separate sheet of paper. When typing, please limit your answer to one and one-half (1 1/2) pages per question (total of 3 pages).

An angry plaintiff, Bubba Smith, has demanded $500,000 damages in a mobile home defect case. He claims that the roof leaked constantly for 2 years, ruining all his belongings. He claims that the problems with the home caused his wife, Tammy-Sue, to file for divorce.

You represent Mary Smart, the mobile home manufacturer's corporate representative, in mediation with the plaintiff. The plaintiff's attorney has just completed a very powerful statement of his case in the opening caucus. The plaintiff reacted to the statement by sobbing uncontrollably and demanding a written apology. Your client, Mary, did not react well to this exchange. She stood up and threatened to walk out of the mediation and file a counterclaim for malicious prosecution because Bubba's demand is "outrageous" and his case is frivolous, in her opinion. In other words, she wants to "strike back" or "break off" negotiations. You think the case should be settled for $50,000 in mediation.

The mediator concluded the opening caucus immediately and placed the parties in separate rooms. Your first task is to meet with your client and encourage her to move forward with the mediation in a productive way. You want to create a favorable climate for the mediation. Applying the correct "breakthrough strategy" from Getting Past No for this situation, what technique will you employ? Discuss how you will advise your client while employing this technique.

During the mediation you receive a call from your private investigator, Joey Slick. Slick confirms that Bubba's wife filed for divorce, but the divorce complaint alleges that Bubba cheated on Tammy-Sue with another woman, Billie-Joe Johnson. In other words, Bubba's marriage ended because of infidelity—not the roof leak. Tammy-

Sue has agreed to testify against Bubba at trial. Your client wants you to march into the other room, where Bubba and his lawyer are awaiting a reply to their $500,000 demand, and intimidate Bubba into taking a $10,000 settlement based on this new evidence, or suffer the consequences in a counter-suit for malicious prosecution. In other words, Mary wants to escalate the dispute. You are concerned that this strategy will not lead to a negotiated settlement; however, you want to use this valuable new information in the negotiation. You think Bubba will take $50,000 if the negotiations are handled correctly. Your client Mary probably will agree to pay this amount. Applying the correct "breakthrough strategy" from Getting Past No, what technique will you employ in negotiating further with Bubba and his lawyer? Discuss how you will negotiate a counter-offer while employing this technique.

Appendix D

Edited Example of a Law Class Syllabus

Casebook:

Rotunda, Modern Constitutional Law, Cases and Notes, 8th Ed. The most recent supplement to the casebook is also required when such becomes available in the University bookstore. The student should prepare all primary cases within the assignments for recitation and all assigned notes for discussion. The student should be aware that the examination will relate to material assigned for classroom coverage and classroom discussion. Preparation for classroom attendance and participation in classroom discussion will be extremely helpful to the student in preparing for the examination.

Hornbook:

Nowak & Rotunda, Constitutional Law, most recent edition, West Publishing Company. The Hornbook is not required; however, the student will find it extremely helpful during the course of the 2007–08 academic year.

Assignments Throughout Syllabus:

Assignments generally throughout this syllabus are referenced to pages in the casebook. The casebook will, therefore, be referenced throughout as "CB." Please note that all principal cases within the CB materials specifically assigned in this syllabus should be prepared for recitation unless excepted by this syllabus. All treatise materials within the subject assignment should be read carefully for purposes of discussion in class unless excepted by the syllabus. Notes and Questions within the casebook are not required for class unless assigned. Students are responsible, however, for all materials covered during the course of class discussion for examination purposes. The assignments for each class approximate the material which should be covered. Assignments may vary, prospectively, as determined to be necessary to facilitate appropriate coverage throughout the semester.

Course Purpose:

The course will seek to provide each student with an understanding of constitutional analysis in the United States, with reference to necessary history and process, and offer each student the opportunity to determine for him or herself the appropriate role of the judicial branch of government of the United States in contemporary America. The constitutional interpretation materials offered for the second class are not for indoctrination or 'molding' of the student's opinion. The materials are offered to provide student reflection, as well as to promote understanding of the opinions of the Court which will be discussed during this semester.

Office Hours:	MW, 1:00—3:00p.m., or by appointment.
Office:	220(B)—Law School Building
E-mail:	cdcole@samford.edu

Attendance Policy as Established By The Law Faculty:

At the beginning of each semester or term of classes, the Associate Dean of Academic Affairs will calculate and post the maximum number of absences that will be permitted in every course. That number shall be twenty percent (20 percent) of the total number of scheduled class meetings for the course (with any fractions rounded up to the next whole number). All faculty members shall record student attendance in every course and report all student absences to the Associate Dean of Academic Affairs on a monthly basis. Any student with absences in excess of the maximum number will receive a mandatory grade reduction to the next lower grade increment. Additional absences may result in further grade reductions at the discretion of the faculty member after consultation with the Associate Dean of Academic Affairs. Individual faculty members may impose more stringent class attendance policies as they deem appropriate, but in no event shall any faculty member adopt an attendance policy that is less stringent than the rule set forth herein. For purposes of applying this rule, all student absences from any course for whatever reason will be considered "unexcused." It is each student's sole responsibility to record his or her own class attendance in the manner specified by each individual faculty member and to monitor his or her own class absences in all law school courses.

Rehabilitation Act and Americans With Disabilities Act:

"Samford University complies with Section 504 of the Rehabilitation Act and the Americans with Disabilities Act. Students with disabilities who seek accommodations must make their request through Disability Support Services. This office is located in Counseling Services on the lower level of Pittman Hall, or can be reached by calling 726–4078 or 726–2105. A faculty member will grant reasonable accommodations only upon notification from the Disability Support Services."

In order to provide exam accommodation, the Cumberland School of Law must receive a letter from Disability Support Services no later than thirty days prior to the end of classes. Because the process of evaluating and documenting a student's need for accommodations can be time consuming, students are encouraged to contact Disability Support Services early in the semester in order to ensure the completion of all necessary paperwork by the deadline. Accommodations received after the deadline will be processed for the following semester.

Examination:

The grade to be earned by students will be based upon the examination administered at the end of each semester of this two semester course. The examination will be composed of multiple choice questions (50 percent), an analytical question (40 percent), and an essay question (10 percent). The content of the examination will be based upon the assignments for class coverage during the semester and class discussion. The exam will not be a "quiz," it will be an inquiry to determine if the student understood the concepts and other materials assigned and/or presented during the course of the semester. Class preparation and attendance are extremely important and should be given a very high priority by the student throughout the semester.

Students may use an outline of course materials which they each individually compile during the course of the semester to complete their response to the exam.

Class 1: The first class will offer an introductory lecture concerning the meaning and relevance of American constitutional law, precedent determination and utilization, and examination preparation. The material which follows will be discussed.

The Historical and Constitutional Basis for the United States Legal Culture, Including Comment Concerning Legal Precedent

The American constitutional culture requires, for both definition and understanding, that one look to the respective roles of the federal and state judicial branches of government in the American legal culture separately.[1]

One must recognize that the state and federal judicial systems in America operate within separate spheres of influence in a manner which reflects the evolving culture of the people, subject to the constitutional norms which govern them. The effects of an evolving culture on both constitutional interpretation and the role of the judiciary in exercising the power of judicial review[2] is a necessary ingredient in rendering a constitution of general norms, when not specifically prohibited by the Constitution[3] current to serve the continuing evolution of the governed.[4]

The material which follows offers a brief discussion of the constitutional history and structure which serves as the basis for the state and federal judicial branches of government in America. After the historical background this introduction will offer an overview of the role of the American State and Federal judicial systems, as such relates to the regulation of commercial matters and protection of individual liberties.

Historical and Constitutional Basis for American Federalism

Federalism, as a generic governmental concept, is properly defined as "an expression of constitutional shorthand respecting the vertical distribution of legislative jurisdiction in the United States."[5] One may further define the vertical distribution of jurisdiction in American federalism as the "distribution of powers between the federal government and the States."[6]

The need for an American federalism began with the recognition that the American Colonies should establish a constructive relationship with the English Parliament and King during America's colonial period. Subsequent to gaining independence from England there was a need for an American federalism between the States and a central government. Consistent with that need, following the declaration of American independence from England, the States joined together under the Articles of Confederation, retaining much of their sovereignty, including the power to tax and regulate commerce, but giving the Confederation Congress both war and defense authority.[7]

The American Articles of Confederation proved to be inadequate because there was no power in the central government to govern.[8] Hence, delegates from the States were sent to Philadelphia in 1787 to revise the Articles; however, they ultimately offered the States an opportunity to ratify a constitution which delegated powers to a central government, retaining the power to legislate for the general health, welfare, and safety in the States.[9] The American government under the new Constitution was proclaimed as ratified on September 13, 1788 by Act of the Continental Congress. The Constitution has been amended twenty-seven times since its ratification by the requisite number of States. The most recent amendment provides that "No law, varying the compensation for the services of the Senators and Representatives, shall take effect, until an election of Representatives shall have intervened."[10] Amazingly, the 27th

Amendment was ratified by the requisite number of States more than 200 years after it was offered to the States for ratification.[11]

The fact that the United States Constitution has been amended only twenty-seven times and continues to constitute the fundamental law of the United States may be explained because it has been interpreted by the Supreme Court in a manner which renders it viable for contemporary America.[169] The dual sovereignty type of federalism which the Constitution created in the beginning of the American governmental experience was based upon the premise that the federal government created by the States was a government of enumerated powers and that the inherent power of sovereignty—the power to legislate for the general health, welfare, and safety—was reserved by the States.[12]

This theory of reserved power in the States depended, for continued vitality, upon a constitutional interpretation which construed the enumerated powers of the federal government narrowly. In McCulloch v. Maryland,[13] a case decided in 1819, the Supreme Court of the United States (hereinafter "Supreme Court" or "Court") determined that the Congress had the power to establish a national bank even though no explicit power to do so existed in the Constitution. The Court rejected the contention of the State of Maryland that federal power could not preempt state power by holding that the powers of the federal government were derived from the people, not from the states.[14] One should recognize that the Court had established the power of judicial review over executive and legislative actions in Marbury v. Madison[15] in 1803 and McCulloch, sixteen years later, established the basis for implementation of national policy, asserting:

"Let the end be legitimate, let it be within the scope of the constitution, and all means which are appropriate, which are plainly adapted to that end, which are not prohibited, but consist with the letter and spirit of the constitution, are constitutional."[16]

Subsequent to McCulloch a federal act would be determined to be valid by the Supreme Court if the act was found to bear a reasonable relationship to an enumerated or implied federal power. In McCulloch the Court held that the second Bank of the United States had a reasonable relationship to the federal congressional powers to "lay and collect taxes; to borrow money; to regulate commerce; to declare and conduct a war; and to raise and support armies and navies."[17]

This recognition of broad authority in the federal government continued until subsequent to America's Civil War, 1861–65, when the Court became more reluctant to allow government interference with both economic matters and individual liberties. During 1888–1937 the Court limited government regulation with a broad interpretation of the word "liberty" in the due process clauses of the Fifth (applicable to the federal government) and Fourteenth Amendments (applicable to the States) which created substantive limitations on governmental power. The Court also used the Tenth Amendment, reserving power in the States if not granted to the federal government, and a narrow construction of the power of Congress to regulate under the Commerce Clause, to limit governmental regulation during this period.

The judicial doctrine described above, using the Due Process Clauses to limit governmental power (generally designated as the doctrine of economic substantive due process), prevailed until 1937 when the conservative philosophy limiting governmental economic regulation lost favor with the Court. The Court thereafter deferred to the Congress and the State legislatures to establish the economic regulatory norms and returned to the principles of McCulloch v. Maryland. Even the casual observer can recognize that the role of the judicial branch of government in America is greatly affected by the role the Court perceives for itself in the judicial review process.

The Court repudiated the economic prong of the substantive due process doctrine which had utilized the due process clauses as substantive limitations upon the exercise of both State and federal governmental power in United States v. Carolene Products Co.[18] In Carolene Products the Court upheld the congressional regulation of the interstate movement of a food product, based upon congressional commerce clause authority, asserting that it would assume that congressional regulation of economic matters was rationally based.[19] Chief Justice Stone's opinion in Carolene Products explicitly asserted in a footnote that there may be a more narrow scope for operation of the presumption of constitutionality of congressional regulation when government seeks to infringe upon individual rights such as those found in the Bill of Rights, restricts political processes, or prejudices discrete and insular minorities.[20] Criticism has been leveled against the Court and commentators for asserting a footnote as the basis for the continued use of the "liberty" concepts of the Fifth and Fourteenth Amendments to protect individual liberties, as opposed to economic regulation. One should recognize, however, that the repudiation of substantive economic due process, treating the subject matter of economic regulation in Carolene Products, should reasonably limit the precedential effect of the opinion to matters involving economic regulation only.

There are numerous reasons for federal supremacy vis-à-vis the States in contemporary America. One could begin by recognizing the need for a national and international market, as evidenced by a broad construction of the powers of the federal Congress pursuant to the Interstate Commerce Clause.[21] A broad construction of the Commerce Clause and the federal power of taxation[22] established a basis for broad national power, leaving the States to operate within a sphere of influence defined by the body politic.[23]

More importantly, however, one must recognize that the Framers of the United States Constitution clearly intended for the federal government to be supreme when it was operating within its sphere of influence. The Framers provided for that federal supremacy with a clause in the Constitution which provides that:

"This Constitution, and the Laws of the United States which shall be made in Pursuance thereof; and all Treaties made, or which shall be made, under the Authority of the United States, shall be the supreme Law of the Land; and the Judges in every State shall be bound thereby, any Thing in the Constitution or Laws of any State to the Contrary notwithstanding."[24]

A cursory reading of the above quoted clause, the "Supremacy Clause," compels one to recognize that the Constitution renders federal law supreme. Federal law includes the Constitution, laws enacted pursuant to the Constitution and treaties made under the authority of the United States. Hence, a law enacted by the Congress, pursuant to an enumerated or implied constitutional power, constitutes the supreme law of the United States when approved by the President.

Notwithstanding the structure providing for federal supremacy enumerated above, state judicial systems in America continue to have a vital role to play in the administration of justice in both criminal and civil matters. If the state court decides the case purely on state grounds then the decision of the state court of last resort is final.[25]

Indicative of the contemporary viability of state court decisions, a former member of the United States Supreme Court, Justice William J. Brennan, Jr., responded to a question concerning the Court's finest achievement during his 34-year tenure as:

"the emphasis on individual rights and their protection—their definition and their protection. That, in my view, has been the principal contribution to jurisprudence that the Court has made in my time, including things like supporting the extension of protections to state decisions that rely on state constitutions rather than on the federal constitution."[26]

The foregoing general descriptions of the spheres of influence of federal and state government in America certainly justify one generalizing that the missions of the state and federal judiciaries are quite different in the American constitutional system. Even so, there are also similarities in the roles of the two systems. The material which follows considers the roles of each system as such relates to cases involving individual liberties and commercial regulations.[27]

The Role of the Federal Judiciary in the American Constitutional Culture

One must begin the consideration of the role of the federal judicial branch of government in American society by recognizing that the federal judicial system is a system of limited jurisdiction. The Constitution provides that:

"The judicial Power shall extend to all Cases, in Law and Equity, arising under this Constitution, the Laws of the United States, and Treaties made, or which shall be made, under their Authority;—to all Cases affecting Ambassadors, other public Ministers and Consuls;—to all Cases of admiralty and maritime Jurisdiction;-to Controversies to which the United States shall be a Party;—to Controversies between two or more States;[between a State and Citizens of another State;—]* between Citizens of different States—between Citizens of the same State claiming Lands under Grants of different States, [and between a State, or the Citizens thereof, and foreign States, Citizens or Subjects.]*

"In all Cases affecting Ambassadors, other public Ministers and Consuls, and those in which a State shall be a party, the supreme Court shall have original Jurisdiction. In all the other Cases before mentioned, the supreme Court shall have appellate Jurisdiction, both as to Law and Fact, with such Exceptions, and under such Regulations as the Congress shall make."[28]

A review of the foregoing constitutional provisions will readily indicate that the exercise of federal judicial power in America requires that the fact situation before the federal court be a case which arises under the Constitution, laws enacted pursuant to the Constitution, a treaty, or come within one of the subject matter jurisdictional grants enumerated, e.g., a controversy between citizens of different States.[29] The second paragraph of the quoted material merely establishes the three instances of subject matter jurisdiction in which the Supreme Court shall have original jurisdiction and provides that all other jurisdiction described in paragraph one shall be appellate jurisdiction. It is also noteworthy that the last clause of the second paragraph gives the Congress the authority to regulate the appellate jurisdiction of the Supreme Court.

The power of the federal judiciary under Article III of the Constitution is thus limited to the subject matter jurisdiction enumerated in the Constitution in an analogous manner to the limited, enumerated, federal congressional powers.[30] Thus, when the judicial branch of government construes the congressional power to enact laws pursuant to the enumerated powers in a broad manner the federal question basis for review of congressional enactments is expanded accordingly. The federal power to regulate in commercial matters is construed broadly by the Court—for example, the Court has found that the power to regulate commerce includes the power to regulate all activities which, in the aggregate, have a substantial effect upon commerce.[31] The same type of broad national policy has been accomplished in the individual rights arena by constitutional amendments, an example of which is offered in the paragraph which follows, limiting the power of the States and giving the Congress the explicit power to implement the purpose of the amendments.

The applicable portions of the Fourteenth Amendment to the Constitution, ratified following the American Civil War in 1868, provide:

"Section 1. All persons born or naturalized in the United States, and subject to the jurisdiction thereof, are citizens of the United States and of the State wherein they reside. No State shall make or enforce any law which shall abridge the privileges or immunities of citizens of the United States; nor shall any State deprive any person of life, liberty, or property, without due process of law; nor deny to any person within its jurisdiction the equal protection of the laws.

. . . .

"Section 5. The Congress shall have power to enforce, by appropriate legislation, the provisions of this article."[32]

The above quoted amendment was added to the Constitution following the American Civil War and clearly constitutes limitations upon state power, denying the States the power to deprive persons of life, liberty, or property without due process of law and, further, requiring that States extend equal protection of the law to all persons within their jurisdiction. Such a construction of the Amendment did not, however, occur until many years after its ratification.

The Privileges or Immunities Clause of the Fourteenth Amendment could have been used to render uniform the concept of privileges and immunities for all Americans, irrespective of the State of their residence. Unfortunately, the clause was narrowly construed in its first interpretation by the Court in The Slaughter House Cases[33] in 1873.

The majority of the Court in The Slaughter House Cases interpreted the first sentence of the Fourteenth Amendment to create both a state and national citizenship. Based upon this dual citizenship analysis, the Court then held that the Privileges and Immunities Clause prohibited the States from infringing upon the rights of national citizenship only. The rights of national citizenship were defined as including such rights as interstate travel and the right to assemble and petition the government for redress of grievances. These rights were already protected by the Constitution as originally enacted.[34] Hence, the dissent argued, correctly in the opinion of numerous commentators, that the construction of the Privileges or Immunities Clause of the Fourteenth Amendment adopted by the majority left the clause without meaning. Even so, the majority's limited construction of the clause continues to be followed.

The dissenting justices in The Slaughter House Cases argued, contra to the holding of the majority, that the Equal Protection Clause of the Amendment guaranteed equal protection of the laws to all persons in the states, although the majority held that the clause was only intended to protect the black minority from discriminatory actions by the states.[35] The dissenters also asserted that the Due Process Clause of the Amendment prevented the States from enacting laws which infringed upon the natural rights of all citizens. The broader construction of the Equal Protection and Due Process Clauses urged by the dissenters was later followed by a majority of the Court.

The Equal Protection Clause currently serves as the basis for the Court to protect minorities in the American society from the majoritative will. Further, the Due Process Clause serves as the basis for the Court to protect persons from governmental infringement of rights deemed to be fundamental. A right is deemed to be fundamental when it has a textual basis in the Constitution or is implied from the constitutional text as being within the history and tradition of the United States as construed by the Court.

The Court's role in reviewing equal protection classifications involving commercial matters is minimal, with the Court deferring to the legislative branch in such cases. The Court takes a more active role, using an intermediate standard of review, in reviewing classifications affecting non-economic matters such as gender-based discriminations.[36] Further, when the classification used by either the federal or state legislatures affects a discrete or insular minority, or infringes upon a fundamental right,[37] the Court reviews such with a strict scrutiny which places the burden upon government to show a compelling purpose for the enactment of the legislation which is narrowly tailored to meet only the overriding interest which it can prove.

The role of the Court in reviewing potential due process violations of fundamental rights follows the same strict scrutiny, requiring that government have a compelling governmental purpose, in the same manner as the equal protection cases where fundamental rights are sought to be regulated or infringed upon. The substantive distinction between the two types of analysis is merely that a classification exists in the equal protection cases.

There is, however, judicial restraint in protecting rights which are not found within the text of the Constitution, or implied from the text of the Constitution, because the Court does not wish to substitute its will for that of the legislative branch. Hence, when a legislative enactment does not affect a discrete or insular minority, or an implied or fundamental right, the Court defers to the decisions of the elected representatives of the people if the legislation in question has a rational basis.

The Role of the State Judiciary in the American Constitutional Culture

As mentioned above, the States in the American constitutional culture have the power to legislate for the health, welfare, and safety of the people within their jurisdiction.[38] One should also recall, however, that the States must legislate in a manner consistent with the Supremacy Clause of the federal Constitution.[39] Thus, if the States wish to legislate the legislation must be consistent with the applicable federal law.

The courts of the States have the role to decide cases which come before them involving both federal and state questions on a concurrent jurisdiction basis unless Congress gives the lower federal courts exclusive jurisdiction to hear matters created under the particular legislation. Generally, any appellate review of state court construction of federal issues occurs after a decision of the highest court of a state.

State courts are required by the Supremacy Clause to follow the construction given to the United States Constitution by the Supreme Court of the United States. The States may, however, provide greater protection of rights under their own constitutions and thus limit the power of their legislatures accordingly. The tendency of the state courts has been generally to construe wording in their constitutions which is the same as that found in the federal Constitution in a similar manner for both commercial and individual right cases. Even so, when the federal Supreme Court becomes more conservative in its construction of federal guaranties the States tend to find a basis for greater individual right protection in the provisions of their respective state constitutions.

The contemporary role of state courts in America is influenced by the Supreme Court's construction of federal constitutional values, but it is not technically controlled by those interpretations unless the Supremacy Clause is applicable to the case before the state court. State judicial systems in the United States are currently assuming a greater role in the protection of basic societal values and will continue to do so. The federal Constitution should not, therefore, be required to be asserted to protect the liberties of citizens of the States when the constitutions of the States provide the same guaranties.

Judicial Precedent in the Legal Culture of the United States[40]

The Stare Decisis doctrine in the United States legal culture requires that once an appellate court in the state or federal judicial system has selected a principle of law to use in deciding the case before it by a majority opinion of the court, thus establishing the precedent of the case, the court will continue to adhere to that precedent, applying it to future cases where the relevant facts for purposes of decision are substantially the same, even though the parties are not the same.[41] Therefore, "precedent" is the legal rule used by an appellate court in the forum in which the case has been decided, applied to the relevant facts which create the issue before the court for decision. Stare Decisis is the policy which requires that the courts subordinate to the appellate court establishing the precedent follow that precedent and not "disturb a settled point."[42] This principle, applying the doctrine of Stare Decisis to establish binding precedent, comes to the United States legal culture from the English common law tradition.[43] Binding precedent is, therefore, the result of the use of the doctrine of Stare Decisis. This material will, henceforth, designate the principle by its product, i.e., "binding precedent."

The American legal culture inherited the use of binding precedent from the English common law tradition; however, the United

States gradually departed from following the English precedents and formed a legal system based upon American case law adapted from other States of the United States when there was no binding precedent within the State in question, rather than referring back to the English tradition generally.[44] Contemporaneously, however, an American State court may use English law as persuasive authority when no other authority exists.

The material which follows will address binding precedent in the United States, including the historical and constitutional basis for American federalism. The text will offer a basis for understanding how the state and federal systems of the United States affect the use of binding precedent, how binding precedent is used in decision-making by judges and justices, as well as how binding precedent affects the practice of law.

1. The Nature of Binding Precedent in the United States

The general responsibility given to judges is to interpret the law which the legislative branch has enacted, not to "make" the law. Even so, in the American legal culture, the interpretations and determinations of an appellate court in a State, involving state law, or an appellate court of the United States, e.g., a Federal Court of Appeals[45] or the United States Supreme Court (hereinafter "Supreme Court"), involving federal law, constitutes binding precedent if the opinion of the court is rendered by a majority of the respective court. Thus, in essence, a holding of the court which is precedent is "law" and binding upon the courts subordinate to the appellate court of last resort in question until such precedent is overruled or modified by a subsequent precedent.

One must be aware, however, if one knows how to define the precedent of a case and to properly limit the application of that precedent to the relevant facts upon which it is based, one can, in many cases, distinguish the precedent under consideration in such a manner that the formal holding of the precedential case is said not to be binding in a subsequent case because it is distinguished on its relevant facts for purposes of decision. In essence, a precedent of the Supreme Court, during the life of such precedent, is "law" because the precedent determines what the Constitution means until the Supreme Court changes the precedent in a subsequent case. The same treatment is given a state court precedent by state appellate courts as such relates to state law.

The appellate courts of either the state or federal system in the United States, acting within their appropriate sphere of influence, will either establish precedent (where no such precedent existed prior to the consideration of the case before the court) or follow outstanding precedent. In attempting to explain the process of judicial decision-making in the United States legal culture it is necessary to comment upon: the spheres of influence of both the state and federal courts; the historical and constitutional basis for the American system of federalism and how the relationship between the state and federal governments is affected by binding precedent of the Supreme Court; how a court in either of the two court systems will determine what precedent is applicable to the case before it; how the court deciding a case will establish precedent when no precedent is outstanding; and how courts either follow precedent, distinguish the prior precedential case on its facts, or overrule the prior precedent because it is no longer viable. Discussion of each of these topics follows, in the order enumerated.

2. The Spheres of Influence of Both the State and Federal Courts and the Application of Binding Precedent

In reviewing the role of precedent in the United States, one must first recognize that the highest appellate court of each state establishes the binding precedent for cases involving state law. In essence, the court of last resort of each state establishes the proper construction to be given to a state Constitution and state statutes as long as the law in question does not conflict with the Federal Constitution, federal statutes enacted pursuant to the Federal Constitution, treaties, or cases construing the Federal Constitution, statutes, or treaties. The sphere of judicial influence for the state courts in the United States is broad because state courts generally have concurrent jurisdiction with the federal courts to decide cases involving matters of federal law other than when the United States Constitution or Congress has given exclusive jurisdiction to the federal system to decide the particular federal question. Thus, state courts can decide both non-exclusive federal questions and state matters; however, decisions relating to federal questions are subject to appellate review by the Federal Supreme Court, while questions which involve state law merely are subject to review only by the state court within the respective state system.

One must remember, however, in viewing the spheres of judicial power in the United States, that the United States federal judiciary is a judiciary of enumerated and implied powers merely. The judicial power of the United States is extended to limited types of cases and controversies arising under the Constitution, laws of the United States, and treaties.[46]

Federal review of state cases involving federal questions occurs generally when the case has been decided by the court of last resort in a state system, with the state court interpretations of federal questions being subject to federal appellate review by the Supreme Court of the United States. Conversely, when the case begins in a Federal District Court, where a basis for federal jurisdiction exists, the case then proceeds to the Federal Court of Appeals serving the particular District Court and the determination of the Court of Appeals is subject to review by the Supreme Court of the United States.

The decision of a trial court is not binding precedent. The decision of a state appellate court is precedent within the state system for the state questions decided and, when the case begins in the Federal

District Court, the decision of the Federal Court of Appeals is precedent for the circuit. The precedent for the circuit in the Federal system is, however, subject to being overruled by a contra decision of the Supreme Court of the United States, which establishes national precedent. The decision of the Supreme Court is binding on all courts, both state and Federal, for the construction applicable to the Federal Constitution, statutes enacted pursuant to the Constitution, or treaties. The United States Constitution contains a Supremacy Clause which renders federal law supreme.[47]

Hence, one can readily understand how federal law, as construed in a case decided by the Supreme Court of the United States, constitutes precedent on the question decided and closely analogous questions. When the Supreme Court decides a question relating to construction of the Constitution, law enacted pursuant to the Constitution, or a treaty, by majority opinion that construction becomes "law" because it is an adjudication of what the federal law means and that adjudication is binding precedent. The same concept is true in the state systems when a state court of last resort decides a question of state law. Obviously, however, one must recognize the separate spheres of influence of the two systems of justice in the United States. The national norms are decided by the Supreme Court of the United States, rendering decisions defining the Constitution, laws, and treaties of the United States. State courts of last resort decide matters of state law, not inconsistent with federal law, thus constituting precedent for analogous[48] cases in the state system.

3. How a Court Determines What Precedent Is Applicable to the Case

Judges, lawyers, and academics are blessed with a very accurate and effective method of legal research in the United States. The party seeking to research a prior precedent which will control the case for adjudication must first determine the relevant facts of the case and, therefore, the legal issue which must be decided by the court. The legal issue to be researched is the question to be decided, in the context of the relevant facts of the case which are necessary for the court to consider in making its decision, i.e., what principle of law the court should apply to the question which it must decide to adjudicate the case.

In America, the researcher, judge, judicial clerk, or lawyer can utilize either a manual subject- matter research methodology to locate cases which treat similar issues or use electronic legal research methods such as WESTLAW or LEXIS. The available legal research methodology allows researchers to find cases treating similar issues and to discover cases within the forum directly on point.[49] When the researcher finds a case which addresses the same legal issues and those issues are based upon essentially the same relevant facts, such is said to be an analogous case. When the analogous case has been decided by the court of last resort in the jurisdiction in which the researcher is seeking a precedent, that case, if such is a majority opinion, is a precedent. In such a situation the precedent in question is said to be binding authority within its sphere of authority, either State or Federal. If the case found is not a majority opinion it is said to be persuasive authority. Such a case would also be persuasive authority if it was not decided in the forum, i.e., within the State in question or the Federal circuit in question, unless decided by majority opinion of the Supreme Court of the United States. A Supreme Court precedent establishes the national norm for the legal issue or issues in question.

One must recognize that lawyers in the United States legal culture are generally highly trained and have offered trial memoranda during the motion practice preceding the trial, as well as during trial of the case when requested by the trial judge. The lawyers also play a very important role in offering arguments for and against precedents which they assert to be applicable to the appellate courts on appeal.

The court, either a trial or appellate court, must examine the authority of the precedent offered to it and determine whether such is binding or merely persuasive. The precedent case will be determined to be binding when the relevant facts in the precedent case, a majority opinion, are sufficiently similar to justify the application of the same rule of law as was used in the case before the court for adjudication. When the facts for decision used by the court in the precedent case in rendering its decision are sufficiently similar to the relevant facts in the case which is before the court, the court is justified as treating the precedent case as binding upon it if the rule of law applied in that case has not been changed by the law-maker, i.e., the State legislature or Congress. Thus, when a prior case is determined to be a binding precedent, the principle established in the prior case must be applied, and determines the disposition of the case before the court for adjudication. When, however, the prior decision is merely persuasive, the court uses its discretion to determine what, if any, weight will be given to the prior opinion.

The judge or lawyer attempting to ascertain the precedent from a prior case must know the relevant facts which the court used for purposes of decision in the prior case and the principle of law which the court applied to the relevant facts. The precedent of a case is, therefore, simply the principle of law or rule of law that was applied to the relevant facts for decision on the basis of the legal issue or issues actually presented to that court for decision. All statements of the court which are not necessary for the decision in that case are dicta. Further, if the relevant facts of the case which are asserted as controlling precedent are distinguishable from the relevant facts of the case for decision, the court will distinguish the case on the basis of the difference in the relevant facts and find that the prior majority opinion is not controlling.

4. How a Court Will Decide a Case in the United States Legal Culture When Precedent Does Not Control

Precedent is established by an appellate court in the respective judicial system, federal or state. Trial courts do not establish precedent. As previously noted, there is recognition of a "precedent of the circuit" in the United States when a Federal Court of Appeals decides an appeal from a Federal District Court. Even so, the binding national precedent in the Federal system must come from the Supreme Court of the United States, in a similar manner to the precedent created by a state court of last resort. In a manner analogous to federal circuit precedent, a state court of last resort within the state court system renders the precedential decision which is given the most deference as binding precedent, even though decisions of state intermediate courts of appeal are precedent for the trial courts of the state until that precedent is changed by a state supreme court.

When a trial court is faced with a situation where there is no precedent or controlling statute, it then either uses persuasive authority available or exercises its discretion in determining what law should be applied to the case before it. Such a situation is said to be a "case of first impression" which allows the trial judge to determine what the general law should be in such a fact situation. The appellate court is then faced with essentially the same method of judicial resolution, i.e., it must decide what general law should be applied to the case of first impression before it and, in doing so, establishes the precedent which will be followed by the courts subordinate to it (either state or federal courts within their respective spheres of influence). The trial and appellate courts, in determining the rule of law to apply in creating "new precedent," will look to analogous cases in the forum, persuasive authority from cases previously decided treating the issue before it in other States or the Federal system, legal treatises, and law review articles.

5. The Effect of Binding Precedent, as Used in the United States, on Decision-making by Judges and Justices

Trial judges are bound by any precedent established which is determined to be applicable to the case before it for resolution by the appropriate appellate court in the jurisdiction in which the trial judge sits. In essence, the trial judge does not have the general authority to overrule prior precedent. When, however, the trial judge is faced with the application of a prior precedent which has been so significantly eroded by the passage of time, or other precedent cases, that it is clear the precedent would be overruled if the case were submitted to the appropriate appellate court, some trial judges refuse to follow the precedent. Obviously, however, in such a case the losing party has the opportunity on appeal to assert the failure to follow the precedent as trial court error.

As an example of how both trial and appellate judges review the effect of binding precedent which has been diminished in strength by the passing of time, one should consider the manner in which the Supreme Court of the United States changed its majority view regarding the construction to be given to the Establishment Clause in the First Amendment to the United States Constitution. The Establishment Clause provides that "Congress shall make no law respecting an establishment of religion[.]"[50] The constitutional admonition that government shall make no law respecting an establishment of religion clearly means that government cannot establish a religion. The problem thus requires that the court determine what "laws" respect an establishment of religion.[51] The Establishment Clause has, in the past, been construed by the Supreme Court to prohibit government programs which aid a particular religion directly. The contemporary view of the clause also prohibits government from showing a preference for one religion over another or for religion over non-religion. The Court, for many years, has used the test established in a Supreme Court precedent case styled Lemon v. Kurtzman,[52] which utilizes a three-part inquiry to determine if the government regulation in question is permissible under the Establishment Clause. The Lemon precedent, quoted from the rationale of the case, asserts:

"Every analysis in this area must begin with consideration of the cumulative criteria developed by the Court over many years. Three such tests may be gleaned from our cases. First, the statute must have a secular legislative purpose; second, its principal or primary effect must be one that neither advances nor inhibits religion; [and] finally, the statute must not foster an excessive government entanglement with religion."[53]

A 1997 decision of the Supreme Court, Agostini v. Felton,[54] provides a basis to view what occurs in the American legal culture as the majority of the Supreme Court changes its judicial philosophy. The Agostini court reviewed an earlier decision, Aguilar v. Felton,[55] which established the precedent that the Establishment Clause prohibited the City of New York from sending public school teachers into church-related schools to provide remedial education to disadvantaged children with federal funding from a program offering such children tutorial aid. Pursuant to the Supreme Court's decision in Aguilar the federal trial court entered a permanent injunction prohibiting the use of the funds in question for parochial schools unless the academic services were made available to the parochial school children as after-school instruction on public school campuses.

The Agostini case questioned the continuing viability of Aguilar, asserting that it was no longer "good law" in that it was not consistent with the Court's Establishment Clause decisions following Aguilar. Hence, the Agostini plaintiffs sought review from the Aguilar permanent injunction, attempting to reverse that decision and authorize the on-campus parochial school tutorial aid.

The Supreme Court's Agostini opinion noted that Aguilar was not consistent with its subsequent Establishment Clause decisions and overruled Aguilar, a case which had utilized the Lemon test as a basis for the decision. The Agostini opinion looked to the cases which intervened between the Aguilar injunction and Agostini, finding that the changing majority of the Court had departed from the Aguilar Establishment Clause judicial philosophy. The Court has limited use of the test established by the Lemon case; it has not, however, explicitly overruled Lemon.

The intervening cases which the Supreme Court reviewed indicated that the Court had changed its view of an Establishment Clause violation and, therefore, found that the tutorial program did not constitute unconstitutional governmental indoctrination. The Court then summarized, asserting that the governmental academic tutorial program in question did not conflict with any of the primary criteria which it currently used to evaluate whether government aid had the effect of advancing religion. The Agostini Court majority thus established a new test to determine whether government aid has the affect of advancing religion, i.e., "[whether] it [the aid] does not result in governmental indoctrination; define its recipients by reference to religion; or create an excessive entanglement."[56] The Agostini Court then held that "a federally funded program providing supplemental remedial instruction to disadvantaged children on a neutral basis is not invalid under the Establishment Clause when such instruction is given on the premises of sectarian schools by government employees pursuant to a program containing safeguards such as those present here."[57]

The foregoing material should adequately indicate that a precedent in the United States legal culture is not etched in stone. The law-maker (the legislative branch of government) may change the basic law relating to the precedent, the passage of time and evolving culture may render the precedent obsolete, or the majority of the Court may change its judicial philosophy in such a manner to overrule prior precedent and establish new precedent. The Agostini Court indicated the manner in which the United States constitutional culture utilizes precedent with the following language:

"[T]he doctrine of Stare Decisis does not preclude us from recognizing the change in our law and overruling Aguilar and those portions of [earlier cases] inconsistent with our more recent decisions. As we have often noted, Stare Decisis is not an inexorable command, but instead reflects a policy judgment that "in most matters it is more important that the applicable rule of law be settled than that it be settled right." That policy is at its weakest when we interpret the Constitution because our interpretation can be altered only by constitutional amendment or by overruling our prior decisions.[58]

> "We therefore conclude that our Establishment Clause law has "significantly changed" since we decided Aguilar. We are only left to decide whether this change in law entitles petitioners to relief[.] We conclude that it does.[59]

"We do not acknowledge, and we do not hold that other Courts should conclude our more recent cases have, by implication, overruled an earlier precedent. We reaffirm that "if a precedent of this Court has direct application in a case, yet appears to rest on reasons rejected in some other line of decisions, the Court of Appeals should follow the case which directly controls, leaving to this Court the prerogative of overruling its own decisions.... The trial court acted within its discretion in entertaining the motion [to give relief in the outstanding injunction in Aguilar] with supporting allegations, but it was also correct to recognize that the motion had to be denied unless and until this Court reinterpreted the binding precedent."[60]

The Agostini case clearly indicates the effect that a changing majority of the Court and evolving judicial philosophy of that majority has in the adjudication of cases involving constitutional concepts. Such is the nature of the use of precedent in the United States constitutional culture. The precedent in Agostini also indicates that the current majority of the Court is taking more of an accommodationist view of the relationship between Church and State rather than, as in the past, a strict separationist view.

6. The Effect of Binding Precedent, as Used in the United States, on the Practice of Law

The use of binding precedent in the federal and state systems of the United States allows a practitioner to determine the relevant facts regarding a particular case from a client, research those facts and ascertain precedent cases. The precedent cases allow the practitioner to project the decision of the appropriate trial court, based upon the analogous case which serves as a precedent, for that trial court's decision. This projection of how a client's case will be decided by the appropriate trial and appellate courts is called "forecasting." Forecasting would not be possible without the use of binding precedent.

In essence, the use of precedent in the American legal culture creates a stability in the law for decision-making purposes and, further, provides a basis for the legal practitioner to forecast the decision which a court should make regarding cases which that practitioner brings to the court for decision. Further, in some instances a precedent will indicate that the facts presented to the lawyer for review do not serve as a basis for a valid cause of action in the jurisdiction in question. Hence, the ability to forecast the action which the trial and appellate courts should take regarding a particular fact situation can avoid the necessity to litigate repetitive fact situations which do not constitute a basis for judicial relief.

7. Conclusions Regarding Binding Precedent in the United States

The use of binding precedent in the United States legal culture, both in the State and Federal justice systems, is one of the most outstanding characteristics of American law. Binding precedent, as used in the United States, provides a basis for law students, lawyers, law professors, judges and law-makers to forecast what the Supreme Court should decide in a case subject to established precedent.

Binding precedent in the United States does not, however, mean that the precedent of a case is written in stone. Precedent will change prospectively when the law-maker changes the law upon which the precedent is based, when time and cultural evolution requires, when the majority judicial philosophy of the Court changes or overrules the prior precedent, or when an appellate court with authority to change the precedent determines that it made a mistake in establishing the precedent in question.

The practice of law and judicial decision-making obtain great benefit from the predictability of decision which binding precedent offers; however, the bar and bench must be properly acclimated to the use of binding precedent for the practice to work properly. Further, publication of case decisions must be accurate, prompt, and easy to utilize. The published opinions must include a sufficient record of the Court's decision to allow the reader to understand the facts which are relevant to the Court's decisions and the rule or rules of law applied to the facts. An accurate record allows persons studying the opinions to determine what precedents are established and how those precedents should be applied in analogous cases in the future or limited to the relevant facts of the case establishing the precedent.

Binding precedent serves the United States legal culture well, rendering the case law acceptably uniform and predictable in most cases, without inhibiting evolution. One must also recognize that the support system necessary to assure the effective use of legal precedent in the United States is, in the opinion of this author, justified by the stability and predictability of legal decisions which binding precedent makes possible.

Class 2 Read the text material which follows and be prepared to discuss the interpretive concepts enumerated. We will begin our discussion with student questions concerning the text material offered during our first class.

2.1 Constitutional Interpretation—Legal commentators are not consistent in the use of terminology associated with the various theories of constitutional interpretation. The numerous proponents of various interpretive models are said to be "textualists," "originalists," "moderate originalists," and, among others, "conceptualists." In considering which of these models for constitutional interpretation one would endorse it is necessary to recognize that the United States Constitution is over two hundred years old and has been amended only twenty-seven times. Many scholars assert that such a small number of amendments for a document which constitutes the fundamental law of a culture is possible only when the document is given current relevance by judicial interpretation as the society served by the Constitution evolves. Additionally, the United States Constitution contains many open-ended words and phrases, such as "due process of law" and "equal protection of the laws." Open-ended terminology requires definition which renders the meaning clear for application in specific cases within the legal culture.

The Framers of the United States Constitution vested the judicial power of the United States in the Supreme Court and such other courts inferior to the Supreme Court as the Congress may from time-to-time ordain and establish. The Framers also created judicial independence for federal judges and justices by establishing the judicial term of office for "good behavior" and by protecting jurists from having their compensation reduced during their continuance in office. Hence, the constitutional text must be looked upon as supporting the conclusion that the Framers anticipated the need for interpretation and that the need would be filled by an independent judiciary which the Constitution created.

2.2 Textualism—"Textualism," as a method of constitutional interpretation, looks to the text of the Constitution alone and treats such as definitive. The interpretive model contemplated here is more appropriately called "literal textualism" because it requires that all constitutional interpretation consider only the text of the Constitution. Supreme Court opinions using this literalist theory assert that the Court is required "to lay the article of the

Constitution which is involved beside the statute which is challenged and to decide whether the latter squares with the former."[1]

Literal textualism means essentially that some provisions of the Constitution do not require interpretation because the meaning of the text is clear. One of the most frequently used examples of a provision in the United States Constitution which does not require interpretation is "No persons shall be convicted of treason unless on the testimony of two witnesses to the same overt Act, or on confession in open court."[2] Thus, if Congress enacts legislation which seeks to vary the nature of proof to facilitate a conviction for treason, one can identify the inconsistency of the legislative act without extra-constitutional materials.

One would recognize the primary benefit of literal texualism, i.e., limiting the interpretative model to the text lends stability and meaning to the Constitution and does not allow judges to inject their personal views into the interpretative process. Even so, as one can readily observe, the literal textualism interpretative model works only when the constitutional provisions are clear, definitive and unambiguous. Unfortunately, the United States Constitution contains many open-ended words and phrases such as "due process of law" and "equal protection of the law,"[3] which are not definitive.

Obviously, when the text of the Constitution is definitive, the definitive text controls. One must recognize, however, that very little of the text of the Constitution of the United States is definitive. When the text is not definitive then the Court must look to other interpretative models to determine the meaning of the document.

2.3 Originalism—"Originalism" is a method of constitutional interpretation which uses the intention of the Framers and ratifiers of the Constitution to interpret the text. A Court utilizing originalism as the means of determining the meaning of the Constitution when the text is definitive would look to the Constitution's text as authoritative. If the text is not definitive the originalist would look beyond the mere textual language to the meaning that the Framers or ratifiers intended.[4] Originalism, like textualism, allows varying degrees of judicial discretion when the model is used for interpretative purposes. When, however, strict orginalism is utilized it is necessary to determine what the original intent of the Framers and ratifiers was in performing their joint task of writing and approving the Constitution. One must, therefore, discover the "intent" to be used for interpretative purposes, assuming the "intent" is discoverable.

The United States Constitution provides that there must be ratification of the document by the approval of nine State Constitutional Conventions called for the purpose of considering the ratification of the Constitution.[5] Thus, one could validly argue that the Framers were the proposers of the Constitution and that the intent of the State Conventions called for purposes of ratification would be relevant to the originalist in the application of that interpretative theory. This same principle, with the Framers proposing, applies to the Constitution's Amendments, i.e.:

> The Congress... shall propose Amendments to this Constitution or on the application of the legislatures of two-thirds of the several States, shall call a convention for proposing amendments, which, in either case, shall be valid to all intents and purposes, as part of this Constitution, when ratified by the legislatures of three-fourths of the several States, or by conventions in three-fourths thereof, as the one or the other mode of ratification may be proposed by the Congress[.][6]

Numerous legal commentators in the United States agree that the States' role in the ratification process must be taken into consideration because the constitutional amendment process is solely one of proposing to the States and, as noted in the constitutional provision previously quoted, the proposal must be ratified by three-fourths of the State legislatures. One of those commentators, Dean John Ely, asserts that:

[O]bviously there is no principled basis on which the intent of those voting to ratify can be counted less critical in determining the "true meaning" of a constitutional provision than the intent of those in Congress who proposed it.[7]

Dean Ely further articulates the difficulty in ascertaining the necessary intent to give literal originalism validity as follows:

[Identifying the many different persons and ascertaining their intent] gets to be so many different people in so many different circumstances that one cannot hope to gather a reliable picture of their intention from any perusal of the legislative history. To complicate matters further, State ratification debates, assuming there were debates, often were not even recorded. Thus, the only reliable evidence of what "the ratifiers" thought they were ratifying is obviously the language of the provision they approved. The debates (or for that matter other contemporary sources) can serve the "dictionary function" of resolving ambiguities ... but that function fulfilled, the critical record of what was meant to be proposed and ratified is what was proposed and ratified.[8]

The problem of ascertaining the ratifiers intent is further complicated by the lack of records of proceedings conducted in State Conventions for ratification purposes. Justice Story indicates that records of only five State Conventions were available and he asserted that we "may not assume that they speak for the others."[9] Professor Raoul Berger writes that: "[o]ne may regard the ratifiers as the most authoritative spokesmen where their views conflict with those of the Framers." [10]

Originalism which looks beyond that which was proposed and ratified to determine meaning would certainly appear to require that the court interpreting the constitutional provision look to the ratifiers' intent, not that of the Framers. Both the constitutional text and numerous commentators' comments indicate that the ratifiers' intent is to be preferred over that of the Framers.

The next question regarding original intent as an interpretative model concerns the manner in which the relevant intent is to be discovered, assuming it is discoverable. The basic problem of ascertaining the intent of the ratifiers, the large number of persons in the many different State Conventions, must recognize the fact that many of the state conventions did not maintain records of the proceedings, as has been previously mentioned. These two problems are, however, exacerbated by the recognition that in order for originalism to be viable as an interpretative model, there must be evidence of firm intent available. The evidence must be sufficient to render the interpretation of the intent asserted as credible. One must also distinguish between the personal views of a ratifier and their intentions concerning constitutional resolution. This level of understanding intent for purposes of an interpretative model indicates the difficulty one will have in utilizing original intent as an interpretative model.

Associate Justice William J. Brennan, Jr., an associate justice of the United States Supreme Court from 1956 until 1990, in a lecture delivered at Georgetown University on October 12, 1985, asserted that:

There are those who find legitimacy in fidelity to what they call "the intentions of the Framers." In its most doctrinaire incarnation, this view demands that Justices discern exactly what the Framers thought about the question under consideration and simply follow that intention in resolving the case before them. It is a view that feigns self-effacing deference to the specific judgments of those who forged our original social compact. But in truth it is little more than arrogance cloaked as humility. It is arrogant to pretend that from our vantage point we can gauge accurately the intent of the Framers on application of principle to specific, contemporary questions. All too often, sources of potential enlightenment such as records of the ratification debates provides sparse or ambiguous evidence of the original intention. Typically, all that can be gleaned is that the Framers themselves did not agree about the application or meaning of particular constitutional provisions, and hid their differences in cloaks of generality.[11]

Justice Brennan further recognized the concern regarding whose intention is relevant for interpretative purposes, adding yet another category of intent to be considered, the congressional proposals as well as the drafters or ratifiers.[12]After recognizing the concern regarding whose intention is relevant for purposes of determining original intent, Justice Brennan pointed out that "Those who would restrict claims of right to the values of 1789 specifically articulated in the Constitution turn a blind eye to social progress and eschew adaption of over-arching principles to changes of social circumstances."[13]

Two additional concerns regarding the use of originalism as an interpretative model should be mentioned. First, the historical fact asserted as original intent does not serve as an adequate basis to determine group intention.[14] Second, one must recognize that there is substantial opinion that judicial interpretation at the time of the Constitution's drafting was more texualist than intentionalist, with judges interpreting documents on the basis of the plain meaning rule.[15] Thus, it would appear that a strong case can be made for the proposition that the Framers and ratifiers did not intend that the Constitution be interpreted in accord with any particular meaning of the drafters.[16] In fact, the Framers' use of broad, general terminology in the Constitution would seem to strengthen this suggestion.[17]

2.4 Moderate Originalism—The originalism discussed in the previous section is that which is termed generally "strict originalism,"[18] which asserts that the Court should follow the literal text and the specific intent of the drafters.[19] Those "originalists" who are said to be more concerned with the general purposes of the adopters' of the Constitution than with the specific intent of those persons are said to be "moderate originalists." The difference between the two interpretative models is generally asserted as follows (material from a treatise discussion relating to Brown v. Board of Education):

A strict originalist... is likely to believe that the Court was wrong in ordering desegregation of public schools because the Congress that ratified the Fourteenth Amendment also approved segregation of the District of Columbia public schools. But there are also moderate originalists who are "more concerned with the adopters' general purpose than with their intentions in a very precise sense." A moderate originalist likely would argue that the Court was correct in ordering school desegregation because it advances the general purpose of the Equal Protection Clause even if it does not follow the Framers' specific views.[20]

Moderate originalism would, therefore, serve as a basis for the Court advancing the general purposes of the Constitution based upon the text thereof, consistent with the general intent of the Framers.

2.5 Conceptualism—"Conceptualism" is a theory of constitutional interpretation which recognizes that society evolves and the meaning of the Constitution, a Constitution such as that in the United States, must evolve in accord with basic concepts derived from the document itself. It is generally recognized that conceptualism "requires the Court to determine the underlying purpose of a constitutional provision and to apply this purpose in developing modern governing principles."[21] This interpretative model has been described by some commentators in the United States as "moderate originalism."[22] Conceptualism allows the Court to treat the Constitution's textual provisions as having a "core meaning" which serve as the base for concepts for decision-making consistent with contemporary circumstances.[23]

Justice Brennan spoke of that which courts do, and must do, in interpreting the Constitution of the United States as follows:

Current Justices read the Constitution in the only way we can; as Twentieth-Century Americans. We look to the history of the time of framing and to the intervening history of interpretation. But the ultimate question must be, what do the words of the text mean in our time? For the genius of the Constitution rests not in any static meaning that it might have had in a world that is dead and gone, but in the adaptability of its great principles to cope with current problems and current needs. What the constitutional fundamentals meant to the wisdom of other times cannot be their measure to the vision of our time. Similarly, what those fundamentals mean for us, our descendants will learn, cannot be the measure to the vision of their time...

Interpretation must account for the transformative purpose of the text. Our Constitution was not intended to preserve a pre-existing society but to make a new one, to put in place new principles that the prior political community had not sufficiently recognized. Thus, for example, when we interpret the Civil War Amendments to the Charter—abolishing slavery, guaranteeing Blacks equality under law, and guaranteeing Blacks the right to vote—we must remember that those who put them in place had no desire to enshrine the status quo. Their goal was to make over their world, to eliminate all vestige of the slave cast.[24]

One should readily recognize that conceptualism is indeterminate and, therefore, allows judges to interpret open-ended constitutional provisions to establish concepts which may be affected by the personal predelections of the individual judge. While all interpretative models allow some discretion for judges in interpreting constitutional provisions, the moderate originalism and conceptualism models for interpretation offer the most discretion. Thus, one should properly consider constraints upon that judicial discretion which exist. Constraints exist which are both internal and external. Internal constraints are those which judges and justices feel obligated to follow and, indeed, in the United States legal culture, the judges of courts subject to precedent will follow. Further, written opinions which offer an explanation of the Court's decision with a rationale[25] and recognition of prior precedent or justification for overruling any such prior precedent also serve as constraints on judicial discretion.

In addition to internal constraints upon judicial discretion, external constraints also exist. The independence of the judicial branch of government depends, in large part, upon the continued acceptance of the principled basis for decisions which the Court decides, i.e., the written opinions of the Court must either follow precedent or explain why such is not done. If the opinion of the Court does not adequately explain why precedent is not to be followed or otherwise follow the definable trends, the holding[26] of the case is said to be "unprincipled." Thus, as such relates to the federal judicial system in the United States, the President's appointive authority and the required advice and consent of the Senate,[27] infuses a political reality into the continuation and predictability of judicial philosophies. Congressional authority to regulate the court's appellate jurisdiction as found in the Exceptions Clause, providing "In all the other cases before mentioned [the reference is to a prior provision enumerating original jurisdiction] the Supreme Court shall have appellate Jurisdiction, both as to Law and Fact, with such Exceptions, and under such Regulations as the Congress shall make[,]" also constitutes an existing external constitutional constraint on judicial discretion.[28] Obviously, the foregoing internal and external constraints do not completely limit the authority of any judge or justice in exercising discretion when interpreting the Constitution. Even so, it should be clear that the constraints do limit the discretion of the individual justice or judge in rendering judicial decisions. Complete independence in exercising judicial discretion does not exist, notwithstanding the interpretative model selected by the Court.

2.6 Conclusion—All theories of judicial interpretation herein discussed allow judicial discretion, either explicitly as with conceptualism and moderate originalism, or impliedly, with textualism and strict originalism. This author favors conceptualism because it offers a definitional approach that acknowledges the existence of the discretion, within the bounds of its definition, and continues to recognize the constitutional text as authoritative where that text is determinate. Conceptualism, and the necessary judicial discretion to facilitate it's use, is also preferred to legislative action by this author because the judicial process is less political and requires principled bases for decision which are explained in the published opinions of the Court. Students of the law should consider the interpretive models described herein, as well as others which commentators offer, to develop his or her view of the role of the Court in the contemporary American legal culture.

2.7 Review US CONST., art. III, §§1–2.

Class 3

3.1 CB pp. 1–14. One should view Chapter 1 as an interactive process between the Supreme Court and American history, i.e., the history and evolution of the United States "completes" the Constitution. Agree or disagree? Why? Can the assertion in the first sentence be justified by recognizing the use of Stare Decisis and the application of the Supremacy Clause (see art. VI, ¶ 2)?

3.2 Marbury v. Madison, p. 1 (1803). Section 13 of the Judiciary Act of 1789 stated that "the Supreme Court ... shall have power to issue ... writs of mandamus, in cases warranted by the principles and usages of law, to any courts appointed, or persons holding office, under the authority of the United States." What is the constitutional problem with this statute? What constitutional citation is necessary to answer the question?

3.2.1 Which issue asserted by the Court is really necessary to the decision of the Court in this case? Why?

3.2.2 What "judicial review" would have been determined by the Court, i.e., a precedent therefore, if the jurisdiction issue had been determined first by the Court? Would the Court then have been required to decide any other issue?

3.2.3 What is the significance of the following quoted material from the Marbury opinion: "[W]here the heads of departments are the political or confidential agents of the executive, merely to execute the will of the President, or rather to act in cases in which the executive possesses a constitutional or legal discretion, nothing can be more perfectly clear than that their acts are only politically examinable. But where a specific duty is assigned by law, and individual rights depend upon the performance of that duty, it seems equally clear that the individual who considers himself injured has a right to resort to the laws of his country for a remedy." (Emphasis added.)

3.2.4 Why isn't the question here political? What is the effect of designating a question "political" rather than justiciable? How is a "political question" defined?

3.2.5 The US Const., art. III, sec. 2, para. 2, asserts: "the Supreme Court shall have original jurisdiction in all cases affecting ambassadors, other public ministers and counsels, and those in which a state shall be a party. In all other cases, the Supreme Court shall have appellate jurisdiction." How is this provision significant for purposes of the decision in Marbury?

3.2.6 What are the bases for judicial review under the Marbury rationale? Why is it necessary for the Court to "find" or "recognize" bases for judicial review?

3.2.7 "[T]he particular phraseology of the Constitution of the United States confirms and strengthens the principle supposed to be essential to all written constitutions, that a law repugnant to the constitution is void; and, that courts, as well as other departments, are bound by that instrument." What is the significance of this quote? Can this question be answered by the Supremacy Clause? Why or why not?

3.3 Cooper v. Aaron, p. 9 (1958). The question: whether there is a constitutional duty placed upon state officials to obey federal court orders based upon the Supreme Court's interpretation of the federal Constitution establishing judicial precedent?

3.3.1 Article VI, para. 2 of the Constitution of the United States renders the Constitution the "supreme law of the land." Marbury asserts that "It is emphatically the province and duty of the judicial department to say what the law is." Marbury thus stands for the principle that the federal judiciary is supreme in the exposition of the law of the Constitution, and "that principle has ever since been respected by this Court and the Country as a permanent and indispensable feature of our constitutional system."

3.3.2 The Cooper opinion asserts "[t]he interpretation of the Fourteenth Amendment enunciated by this Court in the Brown case is the supreme law of the land, and article VI of the Constitution makes it of binding effect on the States "anything in the constitution or laws of any State to the contrary notwithstanding." Is this the precedent of the case? How should the precedent be enumerated?

3.4 The Federalist Papers, No. 78, Hamilton (1788), p. 10. Why is complete independence of courts of justice peculiarly essential in a legal culture utilizing a constitution granting government limited or enumerated powers? Is such the case with the United States federal judiciary? What aspect or aspects of the Constitution promote independence? What is a judge supposed to be "independent" to do?

3.4.1 Limitations on power can be preserved only by the judiciary, with the duty (per Hamilton) to declare all acts contrary to the Constitution void. Without the necessary judicial authority "all reservations of particular rights or privileges would amount to nothing...The interpretation of the laws is the proper and peculiar province of the courts. A constitution is, in fact, and must be regarded by the judges, as a fundamental law. It therefore belongs to them to ascertain its meaning, as well as the meaning of any particular act proceeding from the legislative body."

Bibliography of Appropriate Authorities for Further Reading

Andrew J. McClurg, The Law School Trip (the insider's guide to law school) (2006), Trafford Publishing.

Anna Ivey, The Ivey Guide to Law School Admissions: Straight Advice on Essays, Resumes, Interviews, and More (2005), Harcourt.

Charles H. Whitebread, The Eight Secrets Of Top Exam Performance In Law School: An Easy-To-Use, Step-by-Step Program for Achieving Great Grades! (2nd ed. 2007), Thomson-West.

Charles R. Calleros, How to Take Law School Exams: Preparation, Attitude, and Success (2007), Aspen Publishers, Inc.

Christopher J. Yianilos, The Law School Breakthrough: Graduate In The Top 10 percent Of Your Class, Even If You're Not A First-Rate Student (2005), Career Press.

David Hricik, Law School Basics (2000), Nova Press.

The Editors of JD Jungle, The JD Jungle Law School Survival Guide (2003), Da Capo Press.

Evangeline M. Mitchell & Derrick Bell, The African American Law School Survival Guide: Information, Advice and Strategies to Prepare You for the Challenges of the Law School Experience (2006), Hope's Promise Publishing.

Gary A. Munneke, How to Succeed in Law School (4th ed. 2008), Barrons Educational Series, Inc.

George Roth, Slaying the Law School Dragon: How to Survive-And Thrive-In First-Year Law School (2nd ed. 1991), John Wiley and Sons, Inc.

Greg and Shannon Gottesman & Friends, Law School Survival Guide (1998), Arco.

Hal Davis, How to Start a Solo Law Practice (2008 ed.), Hal Davis.

Jay G. Foonberg, How to Start & Build a Law Practice (Career Series/American Bar Association) (5th ed. 2004), American Bar Association.

Jeff Deaver, The Complete Law School Companion: How to Excel at Americas Most Demanding Post-Graduate Curriculum (2nd ed. 1992), John Wiley and Sons, Inc.

John Delaney, How to Do Your Best on Law School Exams (4th rev. ed. 2006), John Delaney Publications.

Kaplan, Kaplan Newsweek Law School Admissions Adviser (2000), Kaplan, Inc.

K. William Gibson, Flying Solo: A Survival Guide for Solos and Small Firm Lawyers (4th ed. 2005), American Bar Association.

Larry L. Teply, Law School Competitions in a Nutshell (2003), West Group.

Law School Admissions.org Inc. & Robert DeV. Bunn, The Law School Admissions Guide: How to Increase Your Chances of Getting Admitted to Law School Despite your LSAT Score and GPA (2006), Cambridge Lighthouse Press.

Rebecca Fae Greene, Law School for Dummies (2003), Wiley Publishing, Inc.

Richard Montauk, How to Get Into the Top Law Schools (4th ed. 2008), Prentice Hall Press, Penguin Group.

Robert H. Miller, Law School Confidential (Revised Edition): A Complete Guide to the Law School Experience: By Students, for Students (2004), St. Martin's Press.

Ruth Lammert-Reeves, Get Into Law School: A Strategic Approach (4th ed. 2008), Kaplan, Inc.

Ruth Ann McKinney, Reading Like A Lawyer: Time-Saving Strategies For Reading Law Like An Expert (2005), Carolina Academic Press.

Susan Estrich, How to Get Into Law School (2004), Riverhead Trade.

Helene and Marshall Shapo, Law School Without Fear, Strategies for Success (3rd ed. 2009), Foundation Press.

End Notes for Text

1. Civil law countries are those which base their legal systems upon characteristics influenced by ancient Rome, with reliance upon statutes, codes and very specific constitutions. Common law countries, Great Britain and the United States, as examples, follow a system of jurisprudence based upon usage and customs or from judgments and decrees of the courts recognizing, affirming, and enforcing such usages and customs.
2. See Appendix A following the text for information concerning the cost of legal education on a comparative basis for selected private and state supported law schools.
3. US News & World Report, Apr. 7–14, 2008 at 66 and 68.
4. Id. at 66.
5. See Internet Legal Research Group, http://www.top-law-schools.com/yale-law-school.html

6. See The Princeton Review, Best 174 Law Schools, 2009 (Graduate School Admission Guides) (Paperback, available on Amazon.com) based upon survey of more than 18,000 students at 174 law schools.
7. Edwards, "The Rankings Law Deans Hate," ABA Journal, Apr. 2008 at 38.
8. Id. at 40.
9. Id. at 41.
10. Id. at 58.
11. See The American Bar Association standards for approval of law schools, General Information of the Council for the Section of Legal Education and Admissions to the Bar, Number 5, "Rating of Law Schools," p. 135, American Bar Association, Chicago, IL, 2001, for the ABA position on rating law schools, i.e.: No rating of law schools beyond the simple statement of their accreditation status is attempted or advocated by the official organizations in legal education. Qualities that make one kind of school good for one student may not be as important to another. The American Bar Association and its Section of Legal Education and Admissions to the bar have issued disclaimers of any law school rating system. Prospective law students should consider a variety of factors in making their choice among schools.
12. This material suggests that the "average applicant" is a prospective law student who has a UGPA in the B to B+ category and an LSAT in the 155–159 range.
13. See Appendix B for a compilation of the ABA accredited law schools, with internet contact information for each enumerated law school. See also a bibliography of appropriate authorities for further information concerning strategies for success in law school enumerated following the Index.

14. One long-time colleague said "if a law student tries to live like a lawyer while in law school, he will live like a student when he becomes a lawyer." In essence, debts you "run-up" have to be paid.

15. The prospective law student should consult the most recent law school rankings available if such is important to the individual's selection process.

16. The ABA GUIDE is the official guide to all ABA-approved law schools in the US. It is the only publication which contains current admission criteria and other admission information which is provided by law schools themselves. The ABA Guide Web Store enumerates that: The 2008 edition contains 872 pages of detailed, easy-to-read information. Produced in cooperation with the Law School Admission Council, the Official Guide is the one book in which prospective students can best compare and decide which schools are best for them. Categories covered include admission data, tuition, fees, living costs, financial aid, enrollment data, graduation rates, composition and number of faculty and administrators, curricular offerings, library resources, physical facilities, placement rates, bar passage date and post-J.D. programs. A must-have for prospective J.D. and post-J.D. law students, legal educators, lawyers and libraries. http://www.abanet.org/abastore/index.cfm?fm=Product.AddToCart&pid=529008508ED

17. Best Law Schools: Ranked, http://www.princetonreview.com/law/research/rankings/rankings.asp.

18. Id.

19. Filisko, "How Best To Build A Lawyer?," ABA Journal, May 2006 at 39.

20. See Thomson, Law School , 12.0 (2008). Professor Thomson offers convincing materials that legal education must change signifi-

cantly to prepare graduating lawyers for current challenges and take advantage of available technology.

21. The use of the word "brief" for a law student's written analysis of a case abstract in the casebook used for the course is consistent with the professor asking a student in the class to "brief" a case which has been assigned for class coverage.

22. 316 US 535, 62 S. Ct. 1110, 86 L. Ed. 1655 (1942).

23. Cole, COMPARATIVE CONSTITUTIONAL LAW: BRAZIL AND THE UNITED STATES, 2nd. Ed. (2008).

24. A concurring judge is one who may agree with the majority opinion, but nevertheless, offers additional remarks germane to his or her decision. A dissenting judge is one who disagrees with the decision of the majority. Dissenting and concurring opinions are important, as they sometimes can trigger a future evolution of the applicable law.

25. The Equal Protection Clause of the Fourteenth Amendment of the US Constitution provides: …No State shall make or enforce any law which [shall] deny to any person within its jurisdiction the equal protection of the laws. US CONST., amend. XIV, § 1.

26. A right is recognized as fundamental, and thus entitled to more protection by the judicial branch of government than ordinary "garden-variety" rights, when the right in question is explicit in the Constitution or implied from the text of the Constitution based upon the history and tradition of the United States as determined by the Supreme Court. The American legal culture follows a policy of Stare Decisis, recognizing binding precedent which provides a basis for judges and commentators to rely upon majority decisions of appellate courts in defining concepts such as fundamental rights. This concept and the manner in which the beginning law student should be aware of it will be discussed infra in these materials.

27. See US CONST., amend. XIV, § 1.

28. The Court pointed out, in the Skinner majority opinion, that: "If the fraudulent intent occurs later [after one has obtained possession of the property] and the defendant converts the property, he is guilty of embezzlement. Whether a particular act is larceny by fraud or embezzlement thus turns not on the intrinsic quality of the act but on when the felonious intent arose—a question for the jury under appropriate instructions." See Skinner opinion as quoted herein supra.

29. The reader should recognize that an "issue" is merely the question that the Court must decide to adjudicate the case. Further, if one states the issue in the context of the case facts that the Court must consider to make a decision the student understands case analysis. A caveat to this suggestion is appropriate however, i.e., the law student should inquire of the professor in each class to determine the professor's preference in stating issues for class recitation. Even so, the foregoing suggestion regarding inclusion of the facts necessary for decision in one's issue statements will prove to be invaluable in brief writing.

30. Class discussion concerning the case and assigned reading will offer the student an opportunity to understand that when government infringes upon rights held to be fundamental it must prove that government has a compelling interest (an interest greater than the right infringed upon) and that the statute infringing upon the fundamental right is narrowly tailored to address no more than the compelling interest proven.

31. One can readily observe that the binding precedent, the rule of law applied to the facts necessary for decision in the case, consistent with prior precedent, is a declarative statement answering the issue statement in the brief. This approach to briefing is possible when students recognize the question the court must decide and pose such in the context of the relevant facts the court must consider to decide

the issue. When one defines the issues of a case in the context of the relevant facts the court must consider to decide the case and subsequently understands the rule of law the court applies to decide the case one has the basis to state the contextual issue affirmatively as the precedent to be followed in subsequent analogous cases. As mentioned earlier, if the majority of the court decides the case in the same manner and for the same reasons (the same rationale) the precedent is binding precedent for analogous cases within the jurisdiction of the appellate court establishing binding precedent. When the court does not have a majority of its members deciding the case for the same reasons the decision is defined as a plurality. A plurality decision is mere persuasive precedent. Persuasive precedents are not binding but may be used in a persuasive manner in subsequent cases.

32. See Skinner opinion as quoted supra.
33. See Prosser, Wade and Schwartz's Tort's Cases and Materials (Foundation Press, 2005, Eleventh Edition) 1. This casebook has become a classic and sets forth the above definition in the first paragraph of the first page.
34. The Fisher case, set out above, is used in the Prosser, Wade, and Schwartz casebook, Id. at p.35 to illustrate the borderline on what is a "touching" sufficient to result in the tort of battery.
35. See Appendix D at the end of this text material for an edited example of a syllabus one of the authors used to advise students of both assignments and to provide questions which would be discussed concerning the assigned material.
36. See Appendix C following this text material for an example law examination, including both analytical and multistate questions.
37. A justiciable controversy is a case which presents a question which may be decided by an appropriate court of justice.

38. See the facts enumerated as necessary for decision in the Skinner case, the constitutional law case included in this text, supra.

39. Stare Decisis is defined as "the doctrine of precedent, under which it is necessary for a court to follow [pre-existing majority] judicial decisions when the same points arise again in litigation." Black's Law Dictionary (8th ed. 2004).

40. The degree of close relationship of a precedent to a subsequent case necessary to have the precedent control the outcome of the subsequent case depends upon the Court being convinced that the applicable law remains the same and the facts which are necessary for the court to decide the case are sufficiently similar to require the same decision. One can, therefore, understand how StareDecisis lends stability to decisions of judicial cases and provides a basis for lawyers to forecast how a court should decide a prospective client's case.

41. See comment immediately following Skinner v. Oklahoma, supra.

42. A judicial clerkship is usually a one year job in a judges' office, where the graduate will help the judge do his or her job by drafting orders, managing deadlines in cases, and interacting with lawyers and their staff.

43. Statistics are taken from the class of 2007, reported as of February 15, 2008 by the NALP—the National Association for Legal Career Professionals.

44. The Wall Street Journal, Hard Case: Job Market Wanes for US Lawyers, Amir Efrati, September 24, 2007.

45. One of the best sources of information concerning the bar exam is offered at the website of the National Conference of Bar Examiners, www.nbex.org. Much of the discussion that follows was based on information available from that site.

46. http://www.ncbex.org/multistate-tests/mpt/mpt-faqs/description1/

47. Ibid.

48. All but four US jurisdictions require a passing grade on the MPRE. Ibid.

49. Each facet of the bar is timed. For details of time constraints, contact your State Bar organization.

50. Lawyers are required to cite legal authorities in papers submitted to courts. Proficiency in using legal citations is a must for prospective litigators and will be given major emphasis during the appropriate first year course.

51. First year law students are forbidden from working during their first year by ABA rules.

52. Joseph Story made this famous remark in his 1829 inaugural lecture as the Dane Professor of Law at Harvard University.

53. This sounds pleasant at first glance—a 37.2 hour work week with 2-weeks vacation. Upon further inspection, however, an 1860 hour billing requirement means that the young lawyer has to sell 37 hours per week of time. With write-offs, due to inefficiencies of young lawyers, coupled with non-billable time at work, young lawyers should expect to work about 50–55 hours per week to attain 37 quality hours of billable time. This fact bears out the second statistic above: 50-hour work weeks.

54. http://www.abanet.org/yldsatisfaction_800.doc

55. Why Associates Bail Out of Law Firm Life—and Why it Matters, Kate Neville, Legal Times, November 4, 2007.

56. Ibid.

57. Additional information concerning each of the enumerated law schools may be obtained from their website.

End Notes for Edited Example of a Law Class Syllabus

1. The material which follows, offering a brief history of federalism in America, i.e., the relationship of the states to the federal government, is adapted from Cole, *The Role of The Judicial Branch of Government in Contemporary Society, Revista da Faculdade de Direito das Faculdades Metropolitanas Unidas,* AN09-No. 11 (1995).
2. Judicial review, the authority of the judicial branch of government to compare the actions of the legislative and executive branches of government to the Constitution, is not explicit in the American Constitution. Commentators may continue to argue its legitimacy; however, the concept was established in Marbury v. Madison, 5 US (1 Cranch) 137 (1803), and serves as a judicial check and balance on the exercise of both executive and legislative power.

One of the primary concerns regarding the exercise of judicial review is that it is counter-majoritative, allowing an unelected branch of government to determine the validity of the actions of the elected, political branches of government. A highly regarded American commentator very aptly answered this concern by first citing authority asserting that the purpose of the Bill of Rights in the US Constitution was to remove the textual and other fundamental rights from the political process and further noted:

"[i]f judicial review is always slightly suspect because it is not mentioned in the Constitution's text, majority rule should be even more so because the Constitution seems so heavily oriented against it. Taking the Constitution as the baseline in understanding American government and in determining the place of majority rule avoids such an anomaly. Judicial review implementing a counter-majoritarian document is inherently counter-majoritarian; but such court review is not deviant if the Constitution's values are the major premise in analysis."

Chemerinsky, The Supreme Court 1988 Term—The Vanishing Constitution, 103 HARV. L. REV. 43, 75 (1989).

3. One must recognize that the American constitutional culture limits both the role of the judiciary and the methods utilized for interpretation. The Constitution of the United States of America contains both specific and broad terminology. The specifics, e.g., the age requirements for holding federal office, are recognized as directive and thus controlling. Terminology which is broad and conceptual in nature, e.g., "equal protection" and "due process," requires that the judicial branch of government give meaning, by judicial interpretation, to the magnificent concepts for practical application. Both academics and judges express numerous opinions regarding the appropriate paradigm for constitutional interpretation. *See* Cole,

Constitutional Interpretation: A Bicentennial Reflection, 18 CUMB. L.REV. 1 (1988); Chemerinsky, *The Price of Answering the Wrong Question: An Essay on Constitutional Scholarship and Judicial Review*, 62 TEX. L.REV. 1207 (1984); *but cf.* Graglia, *Judicial Activism: Even on the Right, It's Wrong*, 95 THE PUBLIC INTEREST 57 (1989).

4. This theory of constitutional interpretation, serving as a basis for that which has been termed a "living constitution," as applicable fo the US Constitution, is supported by some commentators and criticized by others. As an example of the support for such a concept one may see ROTUNDA, NOWAK & YOUNG, TREATISE ON CONSTITUTIONAL LAW: SUBSTANCE AND PROCEDURE § 1.1 (1990 Supp.):

5. Van Alstyne, *Federalism, Congress, The States and the Tenth Amendment: Adrift in the Cellophane Sea*, 1987 DUKE L.J. 769, 770.

6. R. BERGER, FEDERALISM: THE FOUNDERS' DESIGN (1987).

7. *See* Lesser, *The Course of Federalism in America—An Historical Overview*, in FEDERALISM: THE SHIFTING BALANCE 2 (J. Griffith ed. 1989).

8. *Id.*

9. The retention of police power in the States does not, however, continue to severely limit the exercise of federal power in contemporary America. The broad construction of enumerated powers granted to the federal government in the Constitution has reduced the legal federalism concept of the Framers' Constitution to that which is now termed political federalism. *See* Lesser, *supra* note 7, at 11. Political federalism may be defined as that relationship between the States and federal government as determined by the representatives of the people within the States that elect them to serve in the political branches of government at the national level. Legal federalism reappears when

a majority of the Supreme Court determines that the Congress has gone "too far" and intruded into the states' sphere of influence.

10. US CONST. amend XXVII (1992).

11. This extensive lapse of time allowed for ratification purposes should not occur again. Congress currently places a maximum time within which ratification must occur if the amendment is to have legal efficacy.

12. *Supra* note 4.

13. US CONST. amend. IX (1791); *see also supra* note 9.

14. 17 US (4 Wheat.) 316 (1819).

15. *Id.* at 403–07.

16. *See* 1.0 *infra* for an edited opinion of *Marbury v. Madison* and explanatory notes.

17. McCulloch, 17 US (4 Wheat.) at 421.

18. *Id.* at 407. Chief Justice Marshall's opinion in McCulloch established that the Congress has both implied powers and the necessary and proper clause of art. I, § 8 of the Constitution to use for purposes of implementing its enumerated powers by reasonable means. It is noteworthy that the Court held that the word "necessary" of the clause was not to be construed to mean "absolutely necessary." *Id.* at 413–16. This distinction in definition thus created a broad base for implementation of federal power.

19. 304 US 144 (1938).

20. *Id.* at 154.

21. *Id.* at 152–53, n.4.

22. US CONST. art. I, § 8, cl. 3, provides: "[The Congress shall have Power:] To regulate Commerce with foreign Nations, and among the several States, and with the Indian Tribes[.]"

23. The federal authority to lay and collect taxes became effective in broad terms in 1913: "The Congress shall have the power to lay and collect taxes on incomes, from whatever source derived, without apportionment among the several States, and without regard to any census or enumeration." US CONST. amend. XVI.

24. *See* Garcia v. San Antonio Metropolitan Transit Authority, 49 US 528 (1985) *reh'g denied* 471 US 1049 (1985). Garcia held the application of the federal minimum wage and overtime aspects of the federal Fair Labor Standards Act to be constitutional as applied to a municipally owned mass transit system.

25. US CONST. art. VI, ¶ 2.

26. *See* ROTUNDA, NOWAK & YOUNG, TREATISE ON CONSTITUTIONAL LAW: SUBSTANCE AND PROCEDURE § 2.14 for a statement of the general law applicable:

"As a general rule it may be stated that the Supreme Court, when it reviews a decision of a state court, only reviews the federal questions and not the state law questions:

"The State courts are the appropriate tribunals, as this court has repeatedly held, for the decision of questions arising under this local law, whether statutory or otherwise. And it is not lightly to be presumed that Congress acted upon a principle which implies a distrust of their integrity or of their ability to construe those laws correctly. (Murdock v. City of Memphis, 87 US (20 Wall) 590, 26 (1874)).

"Justice Jackson later offered a much quoted rationale for this rule [*regarding state court judgments based on adequate and independent state grounds*]:

"The reason is so obvious that it has rarely been thought to warrant statement. It is found in the partitioning of power between the state and federal systems and in the limitations of our own jurisdiction.

Our only power over state judgments is to correct them to the extent that they incorrectly adjudge federal rights. And our power is to correct wrong judgments, not to revise opinions. We are not permitted to render an advisory opinion, and if the same judgment would be rendered by the state court after we corrected its views of federal laws, our review could amount to nothing more than an advisory opinion."

Id. (citing Herb v. Pitcairn, 324 US 117, 125–126 (1945)) (emphasis added). *See also* Michigan v. Long, 463 US 1032 (1983) (the Court clarified the adequate and independent state grounds rule by noting that it would not review state court decisions if the decision clearly indicates that it is based upon independent state grounds while the reverse would be true if the case was decided on federal law or it is not clear from the face of the opinion that federal law was not the basis for decision).

27. Stewart, *A Life on the Court*, 77 A.B.A.J. 62 (1991).

28. Another very salient aspect of the role of both the federal and state judicial systems relates to the function of each in maintaining the balance of power between the branches of government within the respective system. A discussion of that role is, however, outside the scope of this introductory material. Several excellent articles and notes exist concerning the role of the judicial branch in separation of powers matters. *See, e.g.*, Chemerinsky, *Controlling Inherent Presidential Power: Providing a Framework for Judicial Review*, 56 S. CAL. L. REV. 863 (1983); Comment, *Separation of Powers and the Individual*, 55 BROOKLYN L. REV. 965 (1989); Note, *Mistretta v. United States: Mistreating the Separation of Powers Doctrine?*, 27 SAN DIEGO L. REV. 209 (1990).

29. US CONST. art. III, § 2. The material in paragraph one of the quoted material which is bracketed and designated by an asterisk has been deleted from the Constitution by the Eleventh Amendment which provides:

"The Judicial power of the United States shall not be construed to extend to any suit in law or equity, commenced or prosecuted against one of the United States by Citizens of another State, or by Citizens or Subjects of any Foreign State." US CONST. amend XI.

30. This type of subject matter jurisdiction is known as diversity jurisdiction, extending federal jurisdiction to cases involving citizens from two or more different states.

31. US CONST. art. I, § 8.

32. *See* Wickard v. Filburn, 317 US 111 (1942).

33. US CONST. amend. XIV (1868). One should note that the role of the Congress has been expanded by the unique power given Congress to implement the purposes of the Fourteenth Amendment by section five thereof.

34. 83 US (16 Wall.) 36 (1873).

35. *Id.*

36. *Id.* at 80–81.

37. This intermediate review is also used by the Court in reviewing regulations based upon illegitimacy and affecting commercial speech.

38. A fundamental right is subject to greater protection by the Court than economic regulation when the theory of relief before the Court is based upon either equal protection or due process.

39. This residual power of the States is termed the "police power" of the general sovereign.

40. *See supra* text accompanying note 26.

41. Earlier versions of this Judicial Precedent material were presented to a joint meeting sponsored by APAMAGIS and the Santos Bar Association on October 16, 1997 in Santos, Brasil, and the Federal Tribunal, 2ª Região, Rio de Janeiro, Brasil on March 30, 1998.

42. *See* Horne v. Moody, 146 S.W. 2d 505, 509–10 (Tex. Civ. App. 1940).

43. *See* Neff v. George, 4 N.E. 2d 388, 390–91 (Ill. 1936).

44. *See* Edward D. Re, *Remarks Regarding Stare Decisis Presented at a Seminar for Federal Appellate Judges Sponsored by the Federal Judicial Center* (May 13–16, 1975), in the education and training series, May, 1975, at 1.

45. LLEWELLYN, *THE CASE LAW SYSTEM IN AMERICA* 6 (Ann Saldi trans., Gewirtz ed. 1989) (1928).

46. One should recognize that a majority opinion of the intermediate appellate courts in both the state and federal systems of the United States are precedent; however, the court of last resort in the state for decisions based on state law, and the Supreme Court of the United States, for decisions based upon federal law, constitute the binding precedent in the respective judicial systems.

47. The Constitution of the United States provides for the judicial power of the United States in Article III and provides that the Congress shall have power to create courts inferior to the Supreme Court in Article I. The courts created by Congress pursuant to Article III enjoy the independence and terms of office as provided in that article. The pertinent portions of Article III, to recognize the limited nature of federal judiciary jurisdiction, are as follows:

    Article III

    "Section 1. The judicial Power of the United States, shall be vested in one supreme Court, and in such inferior Courts as the Congress may from time to time ordain and establish. The Judges, both of the supreme and inferior Courts, shall hold their Offices during good Behaviour, and shall, at state Times, receive for their Services, a Compensation, which shall not be diminished during their Continuance in Office.

"Section 2. [1] The judicial Power shall extend to all Cases, In law and Equity, arising under this Constitution, the Laws of the United States, and Treaties made, or which shall be made, under their Authority;—to all Cases affecting Ambassadors, other public Ministers and Consuls;—to all Cases of admiralty and maritime Jurisdiction;—to Controversies to which the United States shall be a Party;—to Controversies between two or more States;—between a State and Citizens of another State;—between Citizens of different States;—between Citizens of the same State claiming Lands under Grants of different States, and between a State, or the Citizens thereof, and foreign States, Citizens or Subjects.

"[2] In all Cases affecting Ambassadors, other public Ministers and Consuls, and those in which a State shall be Party, the supreme Court shall have original Jurisdiction. In all the other Cases before mentioned, the supreme Court shall have appellate Jurisdiction, both as to Law and Fact, with such Exceptions, and under such Regulations as the Congress shall make."

US CONST. art. III.

The Congress also has the power, under Article I of the United States Constitution, to establish specialized courts which do not have Article III court independence or constitutionally assured terms of office, e.g., the United States Tax Court. The authority to establish these Article I courts is as follows:

"Section 8.[1] The Congress shall have power[:]

"[9] To constitute Tribunals inferior to the Supreme Court;"

...

US CONST. art. I, § 8.

48. US CONST. art. VI, cl. 2, *see supra* text accompanying note 26.

49. Analogous cases are those cases which have relevant facts for purposes of decision which are so similar to the relevant facts upon which the court based its decision in an earlier precedential case that the earlier precedent controls.

50. A case "directly on point" is a prior case which is so similar to the case before the court for decision that it clearly controls the decision of the court, i.e., the relevant facts and law which were applicable in the prior case are so similar that the precedent case cannot be distinguished on either the law or the relevant facts which the court must consider to determine what rule of law it will apply to decide the case.

51. *See* US CONST. amend. I, cl. 1. The author recognizes that Brasil does not follow the same view of the separation of Church and State that is followed in the United States; however, this example of how the strength of precedent may be diminished and subsequently overruled is offered as an example of how the process of overruling precedent occurs, not to suggest an appropriate relationship between Church and State.

52. Materials concerning the Establishment Clause and the changing view of the Court concerning such are based upon comments offered during a Constitutional Law Symposium presented for the Tribunal Regionale Federal DA 3ª Região and the Instituto Dos Advogados de Sao Paulo, October 13–15, 1997, by this author during the course of lectures presented.

53. 403 US 602 (1971).

54. *Id.* at 614.

55. 521 US 203 (1997).

56. 473 US 402 (1985).

57. Agostini, 521 US at 235.

58. *Id.*

59. *Id.* at 236.

60. *Id.* at 237.

61. *Id.* at 237–238.

Class 2

1. *See* United States v. Butler, 297 US 1, 62 (1936).

2. US Const. art. III, § 3.

3. US Const. amends. V. and XIV.

4. *See* Chemerinsky, *The Price of Asking the Wrong Question: An Essay on Constitutional Scholarship and Judicial Review*, 62 Tex L. Rev. 1207, 1234. The author noted:

   Originalism is a theory that "accords binding authority to the text of the Constitution or the intention of its adopters." Unlike literalism, originalism permits the Court to look beyond the language of the Constitution, but limits it to ascertaining the meaning that the Framers intended. In other words, the meaning of the Constitution is static; the only relevant sources of constitutional interpretation are the language of a provision and its pre-ratification history.

5. US Const. art. VII.

6. US Const. art. V.

7. *See* Ely, *Constitutional Interpretivism: Its Allure and Impossibility*, 53 Ind. L. J. 399, 419; *see also* Powell, *The Original Understanding of Original Intent*, 98 Harv. L. Rev. 885, 888 (1985) wherein the author asserts that: "the original intent relevant to constitutional discourse [in the late 18th and early 19th centuries] was not that of the Philadelphia Framers, but rather that of the parties to the constitutional compacts—the States

as political entities," as quoted in Cole, *Constitutional Interpretation: A Bicentennial Reflection,* 18 Cumb. L. Rev. 1 (1988).

8. Ely, *Supra* note 7, at 419.
9. *See* 1 J. Story, COMMENTARIES ON THE CONSTITUTION OF THE UNITED STATES, at 288–89.
10. Berger, *Original Intention in Historical Prospective,* 54 Geo. Wash. L. Rev. 296, 321 (1986).
11. 27 S.Tex. L.J. 433, 435 (1986).
12. *Id.*
13. *Id* at 436.
14. Dworkin, *The Forum of Principle,* 56 N.Y.U. L. Rev. 469, 481(1981).
15. Cole, *Constitutional Interpretation: A Bicentennial Reflection,* 18 Cumb. L. Rev. 1, 18 (1988).
16. *Id.*
17. *Id.*
18. Chemerinsky, CONSTIUTIONAL LAW PRINCIPLES AND POLICIES, 19 (1997).
19. Brest, *The Misconceived Quest for the Original Understanding,* 60 B.U. L. Rev. 204, 205 (1980).
20. Chemerinsky, *Supra* note 18.
21. Chemerinsky, *The Price of Asking the Wrong Question: An Essay on Constitutional Scholarship and Judicial Review,* 62 Tex. L. Rev. 1207, 1234 (1984).
22. Brest, *Supra* note 19, at 231.
23. *See* Cole, *Constitutional Interpretation: A Bicentennial Reflection,* 18 Cumb. L. Rev. 1, 21 (1988). *See* also Lusky, *By What Right?* 21

(1975), wherein Lusky asserts that the Court does legitimately revise the Constitution from time-to-time when acting pursuant to implied judicial power. This implied power is consistent with conceptualism as follows:

One perpetuates no violence upon logic or known historical fact by assuring that the Founding Fathers intended ... to empower the Court to serve as the Founders' surrogate for the indefinite future ... interpreting the Constitution not as they themselves would have directed if they had been consulted in 1787, but as is forthright by men who accept the Founders political philosophy—their commitment to self-government and the open society—and considered themselves obligated to effectuate that philosophy in the America of their own day. *Id.*

Professor Lusky recognized the risk that courts would not feel bound to follow precedent with such an interpretative scheme; however, he cited the changing nature of our society and the need to avoid artificial interpretation of the constitutional text as a sufficient need for an honest interpretative policy, and "cast [his] vote in favor of accepting that risk." *Id.* at 349–50.

24. Brennan, *Supra* note 11, at 438.

25. "Rationale" should be defined as the part of the Court's decision which explains why the Court decided as it did. The Court's reasoning provides the grounds on which future litigants or Courts will predict or defend similar results.

26. "Holding" should be defined as the Court's response to the legal issue presented for resolution.

27. US Const. art. II, § 2.

28. US Const. art. III, § 2.